SO THIS IS LIFE...

Alexandria Goodall

SO THIS IS LIFE...

tellwell

Tellwell Talent
www.tellwell.ca

ISBN
978-0-2288-2451-0 (Hardcover)
978-0-2288-2450-3 (Paperback)
978-0-2288-2452-7 (eBook)

Table of Contents

ACKNOWLEDGEMENTS

Thank you to anyone and everyone that has come across my path in the past three years. The experiences we've shared together have inspired my passion for the written word. Without you, this book would have ceased to exist. Here's to the people and places I've fallen in love with on my travels. To the ladies of *Ochre House Retreat* in Newfoundland for teaching me the importance of creativity and self-discovery. To the many faces I met during my time spent in Ireland, Scotland, and Iceland. I will never forgot your welcoming arms, energizing ways of life, and overall kindness. Here's to the unfailing supports that led to the completion of my book. First and foremost, I would like to give a special thanks to my mother for the endless nights of reading and editing and for her unfailing encouragement and love. Thank you for being my rock throughout the creative process and life as a whole. To my dear friend Clara Lochner for always reminding me to keep it real. Your bright smile and unwavering joy for life are contagious! To the man who inspired me to write the chapter "Lost & Found," Will Chesney. Thank you for supporting me on my summer journey overseas to finish my book and, most importantly, for flying to Iceland to be the cherry on top of a great adventure. Finally, thank you to my family and friends along the way that helped in the making of *So This Is Life....*

THE HYPOTHETICALS

We fall for the pattern.
Fall for what others tell us to be.
Fall for what we believe to be right.
Fall for what science allows us to make sense of.
But what if we were given a blank slate.
Not necessarily an absolute fresh start, but a change of scenery.
No expectations from our normal life.
"A fish out of water."
No knowledge or understanding of what is to come.
How to act.
What it needs to become.
Whether it will survive or suffocate in its new environment.
Maybe it might, if it really wanted to.
We do not know our limits until they are tested.
Finding yourself can only be accomplished when one removes themselves from their existing life that makes up who they believe themselves to be.
People.
Places.
Objects.
Surroundings.
Et cetera.
That is when you truly have the ability to find yourself.

I am searching.
Trying to find a meaning to all of this.
I know there is one, and I am on the path to finding it.
But what is it?
Love?
Happiness?
Contentedness?
Success?
I find myself constantly getting lost on the journey.
Tangled up in the fake love, lies, pain, dramatics, agony.
And then I slowly untangle and find my way back to the path.
The question is: Will I ever know where I am headed?

The idea of the "what if" is always at play.
What if I stood up to the bullies of the girl who just committed suicide?
What if I was born into a family suffering in poverty?
What if I won the lottery?
What if I attended the school that lost five students to a shooting?
What if the world ended tomorrow?
What if...
Sure, all of these situations could have, or may still, happen.
But you never truly know.
The unknown has this insane way of controlling our lives.
It forces us to hesitate before our every move.
It encourages us to chase unrealistic goals.
It leaves a burden of regret hanging over our shoulders.
It's funny to think that two simple words like "what if"
can lead to so many unanswered questions.
Answers that we may never be exposed to in our lifetime,
no matter how hard we may try to reveal them.

I'm second guessing.
Can't see right from wrong.
Unsure my choices will give me the best possible outcome.
Is this really what I want to do for the rest of my life?
It might be a little too late to turn back.
And if I turn back, will I regret it over time?
Maybe it's all in my head.
I'm over-thinking the possibilities.
It's difficult to follow your gut when it's telling you a million different things.
If I let go, will I find something better?
Or do I settle with what I have?
When do I know this is where I belong?
Could it be that I may never settle?

It's a scary world out there.
I find myself constantly questioning others, driven by my fear from within.
Do they have a secret motive waiting to reveal itself?
Am I just a game they decided to play?
Can I trust that their intentions are pure?
Trust is a tricky concept to master.
Maybe master isn't the proper word to use,
because trust will not always be consistent.
Sometimes we allow ourselves to trust others, only to find out they were waiting patiently for the perfect moment to stab us in the back.
Although this is often the reality of our society, we cannot blame the backstabber, because we all have a stash of knives stored away for safekeeping.
The assumption is automatically made that weapons will be drawn.
It is simply a matter of who strikes first.
Or is it?
What if we chose to surrender our weapons in the name of peace?
What if we chose to take a chance on trust in the name of hope?
What if we accepted that downfalls were worth
the unparalleled beauties in the name of love?

Expectations are something I have come to expect to be broken.
That is why I choose not to set them.
I choose not to be disappointed time and time again.
I choose not to wait for something that may never come.
I choose not to shame myself for the goal I failed to reach.
I choose to be open to the possibilities, both good and bad.
I choose to stop fighting the moments I had hoped would come, but never did.
I choose to live without a final destination.
Instead, I live with a praise for the present.

Fear can consume a person.
It taunts and plays with one's mind.
Not because it has any control over you, but because you allow it to.
You allowed it to make you believe that this outcome could never be a good one.
You allowed it to convince you that the small possibility of pain
is actually guaranteed.
But isn't there always going to be a risk?
A risk that you will get hurt or reach a point of absolute failure?
You are vulnerable to anything and everything that exists in this world,
whether it is right beside you or millions of miles away.
Things happen; it's unavoidable sometimes.
So why should we have to let fear get in our way?
Fear is a never-ending mind game, but it doesn't have to be.
We control where we go in life, not fear.

What great weather we've been having!
I know, hopefully it stays around for a while.
A conversation that dates back to the age of the cave man.
Whether you are five or fifty, white or black, male or female,
the weather remains a hot topic for all.
It is universal.
Predictable.
Unbiased.
One of the few talking points left on this Earth that acts to avoid confrontation.
What is there to debate about something we cannot control?
Although we bicker about the likelihood of what is to come,
at the end of the day, the sky will have the final say.
A concept untouched by the power of man.

Have you ever wondered what the universe looked like
before it became the universe?
I imagine nothing more than white and completely empty space.
Endless amounts of nothing that somehow turned into a something.
A something that consists of never-ending stars and unanswered questions.
Scientists and religious groups have their own beliefs
as to how our world came to be, but what about everything else?
A universe does not simply appear out of thin air... or does it?
No one really knows.
Was it formed in the same way that a blank canvas
is transformed into a beautiful piece of art?
Or was it always present and as ancient as time itself?
Is it as infinite as there are numbers to count?
Will we one day encounter other forms of life with similar questions?
Or are we truly alone in this huge playground that has been entrusted to us?
A masterpiece that has no end to the length that it covers
or amount of time it has existed.
And if there is no final point of existence, was there ever a beginning point?
A point in which this interconnected universe
grew from nothing into something.
And where do we fit into all of it?
Are we like the stars that decorate the night sky?
Or are we as vibrant and lifegiving as the sun?
Maybe we are nothing more than a silent whisper of wind
waiting to be heard by the universe.
Waiting patiently for it to speak back to us
so that it might share its deepest secrets and mysterious ways.

We were all born with outrageously curious minds.
Always feeding our brains with answers.
I wonder why it is that our minds are so desperately
in need of an answer to absolutely everything.
Why are we constantly questioning the world around us?
Why are we unsatisfied until we reach a solution or point of reason?
Why can't we simply be content with what we already know?
Yet here I am,
questioning why we have all of these questions in the first place...
Maybe life is not all about finding the answers.
Maybe it is about the beauty of the mystery.

Adventure is not always about following a plan.
It's about taking on the obstacles as they come.
In the moment, you may not always like where you find yourself,
but that is all part of the journey.
Being on an adventure means travelling through the unknown.
Sometimes it means hitting a dead end,
and on special occasions, it means finding the hidden gems of life.
Some of the best stretches of a journey are the bumps that lie ahead,
especially when enjoyed with others.
You get to laugh at the mess you just got each other into.
You experience each other through the good and the bad.
You learn to love each other on a new level.
You get to breathe in every unimaginably beautiful moment with them.
Take on the adventure as it comes.
Learn to accept what you can't control.
Find purpose in each and every step along the way.

Death is difficult to talk about.
Difficult because we fear it.
Because we don't truly know what it entails.
Because it challenges our being.
The only clear conclusion is that death will eventually reach all of us,
and when it does, our body will fail on our soul.
The unclear part is if our soul will fail along with our body.
Is death a new chance at life, or is it really the end of life?
We constantly fear the unknown of death.
The unknown.
Isn't it funny to think that we have defined the idea
of not knowing certain things with a word?
We have defined the unknown.
We have created a word to describe something we do not truly understand.
This is similar to death.
We have made a definition for a word we do not really know anything about.
And maybe that's how it is supposed to be.
Maybe life's finish line has no means of being discovered.
Is it possible to believe that death is just a part of living?
Is death just another stepping stone in life?
Imagine yourself walking across a river,
and your only way to the other side is by the use of stepping stones.
When you reach the stepping stone of death, your fate is up for gamble.
Will the stone support your weight so you can continue on,
or will it cause you to fall into the river completely?
Maybe life isn't about reading into the stepping stones.
A river has land on either side of it.
A beginning and an end to the stepping stones.
We see two sides to the river, but we only see them.
We cannot conclude what they entail.
We do not know if the other side of the river will reveal another river with more stepping stones, a pasture of flowers, a forest up in flames,
or possibly nothing at all.
We all want and hope for either the pasture or more stepping stones,
but that will never be guaranteed.
We need to simply have faith in life that we will continue to live on.
Live your life being aware of the unknown of death without actually fearing it.
Live as if life will go on,
because who knows... it just might.

The end.
The end of a good book.
The end of a long journey.
The end of a beautiful life.
Endings are never easy.
Not necessarily because something ends,
but rather because of what is to come.
Will Tolkien publish again, or is that the last I'll hear from Mr. Bilbo Baggins?
What lies ahead now that I have reached the mountain's summit?
Is there really a heaven up there for me to call home?
Could this really be the end?
Although we question endings,
they will always serve a purpose.
In order to understand the significance of the hobbit's quest,
we must seek out our own adventures beyond the confines of routine.
If we are to appreciate the climb, we must descend to the ground's surface
in order to see the heights of our achievement.
If we are to fully live,
we must accept that death is the only true means of defining one's life.
The end is never truly the end.
It is simply a new beginning.

I'm lost.
I think I always have been.
But I want to be found.
I need a sense of direction.
And I'm not talking about a set of coordinates on a map or a street address.
It is something I need to discover.
Something not even the most glorified explorer would be able to find,
because it is I, and I alone, who has the ability to discover it.
If only I knew what it was I so desperately seek.
But as I sit here and allow the curiosity to ooze out of my fingers,
I begin to realize that the answer has been in front of me this entire time.
Could it be that I am meant to be eternally astray?
Maybe my path is defined by my ability to remain unconditionally lost.
I neglected a rich part of who I was and am as an individual
because I wrongly accused it to be flawed.
I pushed myself countless times to search for something worth being found.
But with each attempt, I found myself further and further away from the answer.
I say it is time I take a chance on my lost self.
It's time I set myself free to run with the wind.
To run so far that, when I look back, I won't be able
to see what I was running away from in the first place.

I am unable to determine when my final breath will occur.
If I will have any regrets or unfinished business.
Who I forgot to say "I love you" to.
What dreams I never got to accomplish.
Where I wish I could have set foot.
I cannot answer when death will come to me.
I can answer how I choose to live while I still can.
I choose to live with all that I've got.
I choose to live with a spontaneous outlook.
I choose to live with love.
I choose to live as if I were dying.

The future that awaits.
It holds promise for change.
It holds untouched time.
Most of all, it holds mystery.
Learn from the past.
Live in the present.
Stress less about the future.
No matter the extent of one's ability to plan,
the future always finds a way of surprising us.
It would be as if you were trying to solve a puzzle with missing pieces.
This is one of those worn-out puzzles you find in the bottom of your old closet.
The cardboard box surrounding it is plain
and shows no sign of what the final picture will be.
And without those missing pieces,
you can only guess what the final image will reveal.
Then one day you find one of the missing pieces under your couch.
And as the years go by,
you find more and more of these pieces in the most peculiar of places.
Finally, you find the last piece days before your last day ever.
When you look at the complete puzzle,
you see an image of yourself all of those years ago opening that very puzzle box.
You remember all of the potential you saw in this box.
Your hopes that the final image would reveal a mesmerizing sunset.
I mean, isn't that what everyone wishes for?
And see that's the thing...
Maybe you shouldn't have spent your entire life obsessing over the puzzle.
Maybe you should have focused on the pieces you already had.
When you reflect on your life and everything you did with it,
what do you want to see?
Unfortunately for the puzzle maker,
they realized far too late that they wished their life away
waiting to be in the future.
Instead, we need to take on life as it comes.
Enjoying each and every moment.
Even becoming a piece in someone else's puzzle.
Reflect on the past pieces you have already collected.
Live fiercely and extraordinarily in the present.
And look forward to the future and the completed puzzle that awaits,
knowing that the journey toward it is just as amazing as the final destination.

TALL TALES OF THE (NOT SO MIGHTY) FAUCET

Do you ever feel like a faucet?
Water continues to flow out of you with no means of stopping.
You are unable to turn your knob off to stop the water from rushing out,
because faucets do not have minds of their own.
So you continue to drip and drop, and drip and drop, and drip and drop.
Time goes by and your once beautifully silver metal begins to rust.
The people around you have the power to turn you off,
yet they continue to let you drain.
They are using you for all you've got,
so the water continues to flow.
They know that keeping you turned on is not environmentally friendly.
Abuses your purpose.
They also know it is convenient for them
to always have the water readily available.
Without hesitation.
The people you hoped you could rely on
to switch off the water leave you stranded.
Unable to ignore the trend set by others.
It is easier for them this way,
even though they know you are suffering from their guilty pleasure.
The faucet has no means of becoming more than what it truly is.
A piece of curved metal connected to a sink.
A sink that is anchored to a building.
A building that is rooted in the ground.
Faucets were not engineered to move on or to do what is best for themselves.
But by now I hope you know I'm not really talking about faucets at all.

Life is a balance beam.
Testing our limits,
as do gymnasts when attempting to master a new trick on the beam.
Pulling themselves back on to the beam with each fall.
The opposing force of life fights back,
pushing them down like gravity.
So they push back.
Eager to land the perfect jump.
Unable to let go of the dream.
That is, until they do.
Falling to the ground until they decide they can fall no longer.
Unable to find the strength from within to persevere.
This is what draws the line between an athlete and a champion.
The difference between what could be and what will be.
To choose a life driven by safety or adaptation.
Do you have what it takes?
Do you have the determination to reach the moment when
you stand in front of a crowd and the judges' panel and land that trick,
knowing that all those failures were worth this one victory?

You are never truly alone.
You are always somewhere.
You are never nowhere.
No matter how abandoned or alone you may feel.
There will always be a path to choose.
It does not have to be right or wrong.
Right or left.
In order to go right, things must first go wrong.

Crying is a necessity.
It does not make you weak or fragile
but rather vulnerable to your emotions.
It is our most physical form of sadness.
The sadness that slowly builds up.
The sadness that consumes us from within
until it reaches our surface and is finally able to release.

My feelings have blended.
I cannot tell one from the other.
They have become an ugly brown with a slight tinge of green.
A horrid shade resulting from too many colours of paint uniting as one.
You know what the colours look like individually,
but together it is impossible to differentiate.
I'm struggling to determine if I am a bright yellow or dark blue.
The emotions refuse to tell me what bottles of paint they originated from.
Without these bottles, I am unsure what to feel.

Time slips through my fingers like water.
The cracks between each digit work alongside gravity,
acting to steal the liquid from my grasp.
As each drop hits the ground, I hear another tick of the clock.
Reminding me that yet another second of my life has come and gone.
As the seconds turn into minutes, and minutes to hours,
AM and PM play seesaw in my mind.
Mimicking my inevitability in the form of childish games.
Their laughter echoes through my brain as if it was hollowed out like a corpse.
But how full of grey matter it is.
Snoozed alarms, unanswered emails, neglected voicemails, overflowing calendars,
phone notifications, unchecked check lists, maintenance to be maintained.
Time to be had and time to be lost.

Rub a dub dub in the tub.
Or a rather muffled version of this cheery sing-along.
As you listen, ears buried in the sheets of warm water.
Mouth and eyes hovering above, accompanied by bubbles.
Taking in the sound that echoes through the vibrating water particles.
The sounds we wish away.
The sounds we wish to escape.
The sounds we wish we could silence.
The sounds we, instead, choose to hear as would a fish.
Relying on the crashing waves to quiet reality.
Acting to separate the ocean and sky.
Distancing the thick oxygen from the gill breathers below.
How I would give anything to be a creature of the sea.
Free from the noise of those above that inhabit the land.

Do you ever feel like you can't be reached by the world?
The emotions have trapped you in time.
You feel hopeless.
Outside of your body.
You become spaced out,
like an astronaut floating away from his spaceship.
The man's distance between the ship slowly grows
until the ship is so far away, it looks like another star in the night sky.
It is as if you have entered another dimension.
Your body goes numb, but you don't seem to care.
You just continue to float in space.
And then, in an instant, reality comes rushing back.
Everything you worked so hard to avoid finds you.
Some break down, while others resist the need to feel.
But the longer you fight, the harder it will hit you.
Hitting you with the strength of a thousand meteorites.

Reality seeps in.
Colouring the water with truth.
The leaves working effortlessly to fulfill their duty.
Brewing behind the confines of a tea pot.
Revealing the final masterpiece as it enters the cup.
I watch as the steam rises.
Waiting for the temperature to be just right.
The patience fades, resulting in an unforgiveable first sip.
Leaving my tongue to pay for the consequences.
Burning my throat as it accompanies gravity to the depths of my body.
As it reaches my core, I feel a sense of comfort.
With each sip that follows, the sensation grows.
Grows until the reality seeps in.
Until I accept what I know to be true.

It calls to you from the aisles of the pharmacy, urging you to self-medicate.
You listen, picking up the bottle before approaching the register.
Admitting you no longer possess the ability to remedy this recurring ailment.
Investing in a future that ensures no surprise visits from the ghosts of your past.
The packaging warns you of the potential side effects,
but you know the benefits will outweigh the risks.
The instant you arrive home,
you pour a glass of water and consume the tablet whole.
Wincing as it races down your throat,
because acceptance is a difficult pill to swallow.
You wait impatiently for the drug to kick in, praying it will numb your pain.
Acting to subside the symptoms you wish to leave behind.

Having regrets.
A dangerous game.
Twisted and dark and cruel as can be.
It eats away at you,
with no intent to stop.
You relive the worst parts of your life over and over.
You do not have the power to take it back,
so you force yourself to live with it.
You think of ways you could have made things better,
but it will never change.
The wounds never fully heal.
Instead, leaving behind scar tissue.
Acting as a reminder of a moment you wish would disappear, but never will.
The moment you can't stop thinking about.
The moment you constantly blame yourself for.

Do you ever sit there and wonder who you have become?
You reflect on the person you want to be and say you are,
but when you look in the mirror, you see someone else.
You allowed yourself to become this person that may still talk your talk,
but now walks a different walk.
You have turned into an individual that is still you deep down,
but continuously decides to betray your inner self.
And that's when you begin to wonder: Is this new me permanent?
Or do I attempt to backtrack myself to the me I once knew?
Can I accept that this is who I am?
Or is this a temporary phase that will quickly resolve itself?
These feelings are all signs of ourselves refusing to invite change into our lives.
Change is a scary concept, but without change, where would we be today?
Change is necessary for us to adapt to our surroundings, because, just maybe,
the things we thought were keeping us afloat were actually drowning us.
Change can bring out parts of ourselves we never knew existed.
It allows us to see the happiness that can come from letting go of the past.
Maybe this means saying goodbye to a toxic relationship,
or forgiving yourself for a wrong you committed,
or removing yourself from an unwelcoming environment.
Although we did not want to change at the time,
our body tricked us into doing so.
Tricked us because we needed to be tricked.

We are all broken.
We shatter into a million pieces, like glass as it hits the ground.
We pretend to be tough as nails, but we are glass.
Failing to see that beauty is meant to be broken.
Not because it is weak.
Contrary to our belief,
it is because there cannot be beauty without pain.
The type of pain that leaves scars.
The type of pain we try to forget.
The type of pain that never stops hurting.
The type of pain we would not dare speak of.
Is it so crazy to think that our pain is worth hearing?
It may not always seem like it, but everyone is hurting.
Some people are simply better at hiding their brokenness.
They attempt to remold the pieces of themselves
that once lay vulnerable on the ground.
They felt too exposed to their pain,
so they attempted to return to their original state.
Although glass can be melted and remolded,
it will never be the same as it once was.
And, just maybe, that isn't a bad thing at all...

The firefly.
A simple creature that reveals a beautiful truth.
In the light, a firefly is just another insect.
However, in the dark it displays a light show
similar to the stars that light up the night sky.
From darkness comes light.
And without that darkness, it ceases to exist.
Although the dark times seem unbearably painful,
without them, would the light shine as brightly as it does?
Would we still see a firefly and wonder in awe at its beauty?
Or is it no longer treasured
because it cannot display its true self without darkness?
We need to accept the darkness in its entirety if we are to see the light.

Negativity spreads like wildfire.
A flowering meadow fades into a pile of ash and dust.
A domino effect that causes everything in its path to come crashing down.
Starting with just one domino, working its way into the hundreds.
It is difficult to radiate happiness when those around you are beyond miserable.
A toxic feeling that few have the power to escape.
Enjoyment of life is in your hands.
You need to know when it is time to walk away
and when you should stay in it for the long run.
Never let someone control your happiness.
It's important to know when you are helping someone who is suffering
versus someone that is causing suffering for you.
Prioritize your happiness.

You are not going to be yourself in every given situation.
Sometimes you feel more yourself than others.
It is acceptable to wear different hats in life,
as long as you remember who you are without wearing one at all.
The many hats act as protection from what we cannot change.
Understand when it serves a purpose and when it does not.
Seasons come and go.
While cold winter nights require the warmth of a hat,
summer days plead for your hair to run free in the wind.
Know the moments when you can take the hat off
and be one hundred per cent you.

Do you ever look back on something that has been a part of your life
and wonder why you let it exist for so long?
Something that has slowly built up to this thing
that now controls your every move?
Maybe it's your long history or pity for them
that has convinced you to stay by their side.
You feel the need to be there for them,
when you know they would never return the favour.
You forget that loyalty is about being honest with ourselves and those around us.
Believe it or not, it is also about knowing when it's time to let something go.
Do you pretend to remain loyal?
Breaking your commitment in secret over and over again behind their back?
Or do you have the courage to be honest before the loyalty breaks in its entirety?
When it comes down to it, you need to know when it is time to plant your roots,
and when it's time to set yourself free.
Certain soil may look promising at first,
but as you grow deeper and deeper into the ground,
you realize the toxins that lie below.
Your leaves start to crumble, changing from a vibrant green to a dead brown,
until they can no longer grip on to your branches.
The bountiful tree you hoped to blossom falters
in the commitment you gave to this once promising land.
While the old and rotting tree stays in place,
hope is born in the seedlings as they fly away in search of better soil.

Why is it that good people always seem to get hurt?
Those that are living for others and grow roots deep into the earth,
more often than not, seem to fall short.
It's as if the evil around us seems to be suffocating our souls.
We always seem to question the universe
as to why these people experience suffering.
We blame higher powers for the audacity they have to do something like this.
Everyone faces some form of suffering at one point or another,
maybe kind-hearted people are just more prone to it
because we were built to handle it.
We can handle the bad because we would rather it be us than someone else.
Always strive to be good, never fearing the evil that comes charging in.
Because at the end of the day, the good always outshines the evil.

People are constantly picking fights, but why?
We hide behind words to feel like we have power.
If you don't like something, why don't you just walk away?
What's the point?
Threats and harmful words may seem like a good idea at the time.
They build you up and make you feel power over another.
But do not fool yourself, because it is delusional power.
At the end of the day, walking away would have given you real power.
Power to silence the fighting.
Power to be the better person.
Power to stop yourself from unleashing the worst possible you.
Starting rumours and back talking others is just a strategy of dealing with conflict
for those who can't face their own personal truths.
Exposing people for what they may or may not have done,
more often than not, trails back to the messenger.
The messenger that ran on their own agenda and only for their personal gain.
But at the end of the day, what did they achieve?
They made someone else feel powerless and degraded.
And the "power" you think you gained will,
sooner rather than later, crumble into nothing.
We all have a choice.
To make a good or bad decision.
To furthermore act on that choice.
We all have the ability to be positive or negative in any given situation.
And just because you made a bad choice before
does not mean you cannot make the right one next time.
Be good as often as you can,
while remembering humans were also built to act badly.
Forgive yourself for the poor choices you have made,
allowing room to work toward the greater good of the world.

Being the bigger person.
Rising above those who are trying to pull you down.
Because why would you ever want to sink to their level?
The best way to tame the beast is by killing it with kindness.
However, never put all of your efforts into doing so,
because at the end of the day, it is not your responsibility.
When they attempt to encounter you,
let your positivity outshine their negativity.
Hopefully this will act to enlighten them on their wrongdoings.
Many people lash out because of their own insecurities.
Let them deal with their own baggage,
and don't ever convince yourself that you have to help them get it together.
Being a better person is a kind way of throwing their own crap right back at them.
Sure, it is a dirty and inconvenient job,
but it is also necessary.
Necessary for you to be able to find joy.
Necessary for them to take charge of their own actions.
Necessary for you to both move on.
So step up to the challenge, if you dare.
Sometimes you can fight for happiness without having to fight at all.
Sometimes kindness is your best weapon.

Quiet people suffer in silence.
Muffled by the assumptions that we prefer a life lived listening.
Little do they know how much we yearn to be heard.
Instead, time is spent supporting others.
Observing what has been put in front of us.
Attempts to engage in discussion leave us feeling
unheard, cut off, forgotten, pushed out, silenced.
So we continue to listen,
because that is what we know best.
Loud, expressive people find an outlet for their everyday emotions in us.
An outlet feeding electricity to any object that it chooses to plug into.
Explains our hesitation to talk about ourselves with others.
We learn to fear our own voice.
Fearful we may silence someone else.
Fearful we will become selfish.
Fearful that others will not hear us.
Fearful that people will get tired of listening to us.
Do not let our quiet exterior fool you.
Take time to listen to the listeners.

Standing your ground is a difficult task.
People may challenge your morals or push you over the edge
or ask you to completely change yourself.
So what do you do?
Do you cave in and become something you're not?
Or do you stay true to you and follow your own judgement?
Do you disappoint those around you, or do you disappoint yourself?
We are constantly changing for people around us
when we should be developing the person we know we are.
Be you!
Those who try to change you are most likely struggling with themselves
and lack the confidence to be their own person.
They are the devil on your shoulder you know you shouldn't listen to
but can't resist hearing.
Make sure you remember the angel that knows and tells you who you really are.
Stand your ground and be you.

Life is what you make of it.
You get to decide what it looks like,
who is lucky enough to be a part of it,
and where it takes you.
I truly believe we are in control of our own destiny.
You determine what your life becomes.
You may have help along the way,
but they are just secondary factors in your story.
The relationships you form may influence and grow you as an individual,
but they are relationships you chose to be in.
You see something in them that reflects the person you strive to be.
Just like you see something in the places you choose to go,
the new opportunities you decide to take on,
and the lifelong promises you commit to.
It's all on you.
Sometimes you may get caught up in other people's mess,
becoming collateral damage to their decisions, but that's on them.
You get to control your happiness, not them.
They don't get a say in what your life looks like.
This is your life, so go out and live it the way you want to.

Life is one big mess.
The second you feel you have it together, something falls out of place.
Life is always challenging us to change, to face our fears, to persevere.
Each obstacle brings with it struggle and difficulty,
as well as the opportunity to change and develop.
If nothing ever happened, it would get rather boring.
Living day to day without conflict would leave little room to grow as a person.
Not to say you should go out in search of it,
but when it comes your way, do not avoid it.
We all need to expose ourselves to the mess.
It allows us to form tougher skin.
To stand up for ourselves.
To become the person we were meant to be.
Learn to accept the mess.
Find beauty in the mess of it all.

I sit here in tears.
Tears that fall unlike any rain I have ever witnessed.
Rain is supposed to be dark, undesirable, saddening, painful.
Yet I feel warmth, joy, expressiveness, courage.
As each raindrop falls,
I feel a piece of my deepest burdens vanishing into thin air.
The clouds slowly transition from a state of darkness to light,
unleashing rays of sunshine as they part.
They precipitate into something that can once again be real.
Something beyond the agony I once felt.
Although those below receiving the rain feel the suffering associated with it,
how would they be able to grow and flourish as organisms without that water?
As beings, we feel this instinct within ourselves to seek shelter from the storm.
To find a sense of comfort and protection.
A means of survival.
What if, instead, we decided to dance in the rain?

A BUBBLE WORLD

We all live in a bubble world.
Transitioning from one day to the next with little change.
Failing to see what lies beyond the horizon.
Blinded by the rays of sunlight that pierce outwards from the earth's belly.
Although I am pretty sure they invented something for that.
What was the name?
Hmmmmmmmmmm.
Oh right, sunglasses.
One of the many tools we can use as a means to pop the "bubble."
The bubble that stands between you and the world.
The bubble that sets out to limit us to what we know
rather than opening our eyes to what we could know.
Formed from the languages we speak.
Who we are surrounded by.
Where we grow up.
What society tells us to be right.
But how wrong they are.
While they may say to do one thing, they choose then to do the other.
Choose to refrain from exposing one's self from new ways of life
or to learn from those that are different from us.
Choose to drive the same route from home to work every day
or to explore the roads less travelled.
Choose to turn away from the suffering to the comfort of our homes
or to stand side by side with those in need.
Choose to be more than this bubble world.

I see you.
A phrase I have come to know quite well.
At first, I said it merely out of instinct.
Whether it was to the creatures of Faradawn Animal Sanctuary in Ireland or to the cottage children of Scotland that had come into my care.
Now I am beginning to realize why these words continue to flow from my mouth.
To say "I see you" is to acknowledge another's presence.
Three syllables that act to accept another.
This being: a person, place, or thing.
No matter the noun of choice, the context remains untouched.
Acting as a token of respect.
Capturing what lies in front of you.
Who they are.
Why they came into your existence.
How they feel.
Where they wish to head next.
One moment in time set aside to understand another.
That's all it takes.

Your head suddenly starts to heat up.
You feel the sweats coming on.
Your skin starts to stick to your pajamas.
You're nestled in bed, refusing the thought of getting up.
So what do you do?
Not a lot of options due to your rather sluggish mood.
I mean, you did just wake up, unexpectedly, in the middle of the night.
It's 4:00 a.m. and the clock is ticking.
All you want, with every ounce of your body, is to fall back into a deep slumber.
And then, suddenly it comes to you.
Flip the pillow.
Feel the cool material on your face once again.
The smooth new surface brushing up against your cheek.
A rather simple solution to your late night kerfuffle.
And sometimes that's all it takes.
One small and simple adjustment.
We create such a fuss about anything and everything.
Exaggerating over the obstacles we must face.
Never failing to complain over the little things.
Although we may think the issue lies somewhere beyond the covers,
it lies in our ability to adapt.
Our ability to accept perspective.
Our ability to flip the situation.
The most extravagant challenges in life often start with a minute conflict.
A conflict we see as this life-altering, diplomatic task.
When in reality it requires nothing more than a quick fix.
So I am begging you, skip the dramatics.
Flip the fricken pillow and get on with your life.
You'll thank me in the morning.

Money.
A concept created by people to control people.
A sheet of green paper acting to determine our very survival.
A credit card with a code to the promised land.
Feeding our natural instinct to be greedy.
Acting to set aside the rich from the poor.
Encouraging us to take the wealth for ourselves.
Why is it that we have allotted such power to an object?
Living out our lives in a game of Monopoly.
Circling around the board aimlessly.
Moving from one day to the next,
as does a pawn under the order of the dice.
Instead, choose to live a life undefined by the guidelines of the game.
Write out a new set of instructions for you to follow.
Acting to enable yourself to see past the numbers.

We all say things,
because words are just words, right?
That's AIDS.
Wow, how very gay of you.
Kill yourself.
Stop acting so retarded.
With that outfit on, she's asking to be raped.
Although these phrases seem rather serious on paper,
they are constantly taken out of context.
You are lying to yourself if you cannot recall an incident
in which one of these sayings was accompanied by laughter.
We do this as a means to diminish their significance.
We redefine their meaning.
We turn them into a joke.
We say it's all fun and games...
that is until it's not.
We would much rather laugh than cry over our suffering,
acting to bury the shame, hardships, fear, insecurities, pain, sadness
from ourselves and those around us.

Have you ever thought what it would be like to be born as a different form of life?
Imagine what it would be like to transform from a tiny seedling
into a vibrant flower.
Picture yourself growing up alongside a pack of fierce wolves.
Or flying through the air as a powerful eagle.
How would your life be different?
Why was I chosen to be a human instead of a fish?
How do our paths differ?
Maybe I'm jealous of these creatures.
Jealous of a hummingbird's elegance.
Jealous of a wild horse's freedom.
Jealous of a giraffe's ability to see life from a higher view.
Jealous of a pine tree's compelling fragrance.
Would I be mad at the human race for the nature they have destroyed?
Could my woods have been destroyed during a deforestation?
Or my coral community polluted in an oil spill?
You could have easily been that ant you just stepped on,
but you are not... so why care?
Care because life is precious, no matter the size or shape.
Without each other we cease to exist.
Together we can survive and thrive on Mother Earth.
I encourage you to ask yourself what life would look like
as an ancient oak tree or an enchanting butterfly or a loyal dog?
At the end of the day, life is life.
No matter how often we say otherwise,
we must learn to love all members of our family on this place we call home.
If not, one day we may not have a place to call home at all.

It's seven o'clock, time to take your evening Lantus.
Facial drooping. Arm weakness. Speech difficulties. Time to call 911.
Cough, cough, cough. Mom, can you help me with my nebulizer treatment?
No one cares. No one knows how it feels. No one would miss me.
One stair, two stair, three stair, thump. Dad, I think it's time for long term care.
Hold their hand and let them know you are here. They won't feel a thing.
Grip chest. Grab nitroglycerin. Give one to two sprays to alleviate pressure.
Who are you? My son, you say. I don't think so. I don't remember having kids.
I'm afraid the cancer has spread. Radiation and chemo were ineffective.
Can you feel that? No. How about this? No. Try wiggling your toes. I can't...
I am healthy, one of the lucky ones. Take a minute to let that settle in.

Humankind adapts on a trial and error basis.
A never-ending experiment.
Learning from our mistakes.
Each brain thriving on a specific curriculum.
While some are visual learners,
others prefer a hands-on experience.
Certain students determine the value of *x* in a matter of seconds,
while their peers would much prefer a Shakespearian soliloquy.
A person with high test records may have their facts straight,
but their dyslexic locker neighbour flourishes in any social situation.
No matter the learning style,
there will always be pros and cons.
No matter the student,
we all fall and rise again.
No matter the curveball life decides to throw our way,
the individual finds a means to overcome it.
Here's to those that learn by doing.
You jump right into it.
Laying your hand of cards out on the table with confidence.
Taking on the risks as they come.
You live on the wild side.
That is, until the chaos you surrounded yourself with consumes you.
Becomes a part of who you are.
Here's to the observers.
You see life as it is.
Choosing to do right when others do wrong.
Your battle starts young.
But with each step you take, the battle becomes a little less difficult.
The puzzle pieces fit together ever so slowly.
No matter the path,
we all learn.

Imagine a world without mirrors.
A world where you can no longer see the physical being.
No mirrors, pictures, or images of one's self.
No means to self-critique your body.
No possibility to compare your looks to those of another.
You are who you are.
Your surface does not define you, because it is just your surface.
Without mirrors, it is just another piece of you.
Something that exists but no longer has the ability to define you.
Would we become less self absorbed?
Could we simply love ourselves for who we are?
And if we did, how would the world look different?
Would we still be scared of imperfection?
Could we reach a new level of potential?
Keeping this in mind,
imagine a world where your surface reflects what lies beneath.
Your physical being is one with your soul.
Your appearance is defined by the person you are.
Shaped by your actions.
Trains of thought.
Ways of life.
Completely exposed for everything that you are.
Only as beautiful as you choose to be.
No longer living in a visual world but a world of truth.
A world that values a person for everything they are.
A world that redefines the surface.
A world that believes in beauty from within.

True kindness is air.
Not to be seen or heard.
Existing without the need for praise.
Knowing its worth despite the lack of acknowledgement.
Often, kindness is mistaken for pollution.
A collection of dishonorable clouds.
Leaving the once-pure air to rot in your personal gain.
Others buy tickets to the show, filling your theatre with spectators.
If only they knew it was just an act.
A production made for the sole purpose to sell.

Every once in a while we need a wakeup call
to see everything we've been missing out on.
And yes, I know everything is a lot of things.
But sometimes our ignorance gets the best of us.
We become blinded by our own selfishness.
It is sad and pitiful, but it happens.
We lose sight of the life taking place right in front of us.
For some, it occurs when they least expect it.
For others, it appears after a great tragedy.
People see how easily life can change.
How quickly something so good can become so very bad.
Life is suddenly a little simpler.
You see people and places that were once invisible.
You feel every sensation in your body, every emotion and feeling.
You begin to wonder how you were able to function for so long,
unaware of the imaginary restraints you strapped yourself into.
You, as the keyholder, possess the power to free yourself.
You and you alone.

Control is an allusion.
A flawed invention.
A last attempt to stop the spiraling.
A bandage that will inevitably be spoiled with blood once again.
But don't fret, your first aid kit has an unlimited supply.
Slap on another dressing.
Apply more pressure.
Initiate a platelet transfusion.
Whatever you do, do it fast.
You—both the hemorrhaging patient and the unrelenting caregiver.
Trying to save yourself from the unavoidable.
Attempting to control what can't be controlled.
Unable to admit when you must call time of death.

Being alone.
We all need time to be with no one but ourselves.
Finding time alone is crucial for everyone to have in their life.
While some of us love being alone, others fear the idea of it.
Maybe they are afraid of themselves?
Do they think no one will come looking for them once they are fully alone?
Or will anyone care enough that they are gone?
Many of us latch on to other people
because we don't know how to be by ourselves.
That's where many of us have it wrong.
Before you can engage yourself with other people, you need to know yourself.
To know how your own brain works.
To know who you are and who you strive to be.
To know you can do things for yourself.
To know you love yourself.
Before you begin to love others, you have to ask yourself who you are.
Understand yourself when no one else is around.
Become one with yourself.
I challenge you to at least fifteen minutes of alone time each day.
Even if that means plugging in your headphones and going for a run.
Relaxing outside in your backyard hammock.
Sitting in your room writing.
No technology, no people, no one but you.
Although we can learn so much about ourselves through others,
you would be surprised how much you can learn
about yourself by doing absolutely nothing.
Absolutely nothing but being alone.

Do you ever feel like you were born in the wrong generation?
You want to feast on everything life has to offer,
but the waitress keeps dishing out the wrong order.
I love life and all of the potential it holds.
I just hope I can find my high.
A high beyond that of the hippies' wildest dreams.
It is important to remember that each generation brings with it new opportunity.
Although we may not like every bit of it,
we were meant to experience it.
The good and the bad.
Moving forward, I have decided to focus on what makes me feel good.
So what?
Maybe I was born in the wrong generation.
That does not mean I have to change who I am.
Setting out to pretend I like what others say to be "fun."
Put yourself in the places you want to be.
You do not always have to follow the crowd,
especially when you don't like where they are headed.

To be alive.
A heartbeat.
Breathing lungs.
A functional brain.
One cohesive body.
Food and water to fuel that body.
Shelter and safety to protect it.
A steady income to sustain these said components of survival.
They, however, are not what it takes to be alive.
Life cannot be defined simply by our ability to remain alive.
Instead, it can be defined by our ability to make something of that life.
To be beyond that of the physical being.
To be willing to take risks.
To be one with others.
To be open to the unknown.
To be more than this cyclical society.
To be alive.

Time is a funny thing.
Sometimes we wish it away,
while other times we want to hit the pause button.
It teaches us to be patient.
To be grateful for the time we have been given.
To never rush.
Society always seems to be running out of time.
Running out of time to relax.
To be with the ones we love.
To enjoy the silence.
To take a minute to breathe.
Because, just in case you didn't know, time is slowly killing us.
We are all bombs waiting to explode when our timer runs out.
And when that timer hits zero, we leave this world.
At the end of the day, I hope my time was used wisely.
Used to help.
Used to grow those around me.
Used to make something of myself.
Tick tock, tick tock, tick tock.

Walking.
A rather simple concept.
At the young age of one, we go from crawling to stepping.
Learning how to put one foot in front of the other.
Looking to our parents with teary eyes when we stumble.
Picking ourselves back up with each failed attempt.
What I want to bring your attention to
is the speed at which we choose to participate in said activity.
Not to ridicule the speed walkers of the world,
but rather to encourage the idea of slowing your pace.
The final destination will be there waiting for you, no matter the speed of choice.
So why not take your time getting there?
By choosing to walk five kilometres per hour versus twelve, you see more.
More scenery around you.
More time spent with your fellow walkers.
More opportunity to experience life in the moment.

I'm an old soul in a new world.

Do you ever think of life as a lump sum
and wonder who else thinks the same way as you?
Do their actions truly reflect who they are?
Or are they a hollow log rotting from the inside out?
Deteriorating from within.
Were they born that way?
Did they make choices that led them to be so?
Or is it not a choice at all?
Were we all born for the sole purpose of destruction?
I've always believed we have the ability to choose,
but then I see or hear or pitifully convince myself otherwise.
I want to know if other people are as scared as me.
Scared of all the artificialness that makes up so much of what we have become.
Scared of what others value.
Scared of not finding others who see life through the same looking glass as I do.
Scared that I am too different.

During my travels along the East Coast of Canada,
I was able to visit a Buddhist monastery.
I found myself welcomed by the array of monks
that greeted me with warm smiles and waved as I passed by.
On arrival, a quote embedded in the very walls of their
worshipping grounds caught my eye:
"Don't be so predictable."
The monks I encountered that day have
devoted themselves to peace and compassion,
a philosophy far beyond that of society.
Beyond the predictability, perhaps, of humanity itself.
It makes you wonder: In what ways I am predictable?
Wake up, go to work or school, come home, work out, eat dinner, socialize,
watch television, sleep, repeat, repeat, and (guess what) repeat.
The very predictability of my being is always two steps ahead of me.
Not because I want it to be, because I allow it.
I say it's time I flirt with the idea of the unpredictable.
Might even try to get a date out of it.
And from there, who knows what the future holds for the two of us.
One might say,
the only predictable thing about that is the unpredictability of it all.

Why would you ever want to be normal?
Does it truly exist?
Everyone has their own funkiness that makes them who they are.
Being normal is overrated.
Never change yourself for anyone or anything.
Never change the beautiful or damaged parts of yourself.
Never forget who you are,
because you are amazing just the way you are.
And most importantly,
never let anyone tell you anything different!
Fight for the person you are,
not who they want you to be.

How easy it is to say yes.
A word utilized to accept what has been offered.
A response commonly associated with more "favourable" outcomes.
A single syllable people wait impatiently to hear.
What if, instead, you chose to say no?
How would your life look different?
We abuse the use of yes as a means to please others.
To submit ourselves to the pressure.
To fall for what society tells us to be.
To believe that we only have one choice.
In doing so, we repeatedly say no to our inner self.
Instead, make the decision to say yes to yourself.
Whether that entails saying yes or no to others
all depends on the answer you initially gave yourself.

Many people seem to lack appreciation these days,
fostering a generation of complainers when there should be a "thank you" or two.
Youth struggle to find responsibility and drive in their life,
leaving little for them to live up to.
Parents continue to give away their money
rather than teaching their children the worth in earning it for one's self.
Whatever happened to getting your hands dirty?
But no, simply snap their fingers and the money will appear.
Under the impression that grumbles and moans are the key to success,
real life is going to hit them like a truck.

Honest conversations are a scarce breed.
Masked by small talk.
Under the impression that no one will understand.
Fearing they will not be accepted by others.
Never considering what could and can be.
What if, instead of hiding from each other, isolating ourselves, we talked about it?
We have become a society that traps the heart from speaking its truth.
Deep conversations feed the soul.
Being true to ourselves is an essential part of life.
Why would you ever want to hide behind something you are not?
Seeking comfort from the shiny phone screens that "protect" us.
Rewiring our brains to believe life is better lived in isolation.
Unable to see that true conversations keep us connected.
Allow us to learn and grow from each other.
Ensure that we are not alone in this world.
Promise me you won't just think deeply, but talk deeply too.

The idea of being humble is slipping away from society.
People feel this urgent need to share any and every victory.
They become entitled to an imaginary reward.
Feeding off the praise that awaits.
Waiting for their moment as top dog.
Too busy competing for the title to see the small victories in life.
The accomplishments worth celebrating.
The achievements that go unseen.
Because putting them on display won't change their significance.
The front pages of *TIME* magazine are incomparable to their heroic measures.
True kindness is not justified by ego boosting experiences.
Humbleness is defined by one's ability to let their actions speak for themselves.
To live a life of compassion without expecting anything in return.
To fight the good fight from behind the scenes.
To be the best damn cameraman anyone has ever seen.
Well, not everyone... just those you care about the most.
The people who know your role in the making of the newest Marvel movie.
Without you, who would Captain America and Iron Man be?
Two silly super heroes without an audience.
No purpose to exist.
So I am asking you, when given the choice, not to be the hero.
Choose to be the cameraman.

Being an individual.
Knowing yourself.
Inside and out.
Many people struggle with this concept.
They fear themselves.
Fear what others see.
Fear what the mirror has to say.
See, the funny thing is, I have always known who I am.
The scary part for me is not knowing who other people are deep down.
Can I trust them like I trust myself?
Do I believe they are the people I have come to know?
Can they handle the person I know myself to be?
So many unanswered questions
that few too many individuals lack the confidence to answer.

It seems these days that every day is designated to pay tribute.
Birthdays, Mother's Day, National Dog Day, anniversary dates, Family Day, and so on.
All of these days celebrate an aspect of life.
Although these days show our appreciation,
shouldn't we show our love for them every day?
Should we not always care for our parents, our special someone, our dog?
We set aside one day of the year to recognize their importance.
Don't they deserve to be told they are significant
for more than twenty-four hours out of the entire year?
Shouldn't life be rejoiced on a regular basis?
One day does not do them proper justice.
Use these special days to go above and beyond,
but make sure to simply love those dearest to you on the 364 days that remain.
Celebrate life whenever and however you can.
Celebrate with every ounce of your body.
Celebrate just because.
Take your dog for a walk to the park every morning.
Say I love you any opportunity you get.
Get out that old board game and play it with your family.
Surprise your partner with flowers for no reason at all.
Love has powers beyond our imagination.
Take time each day to love life and everything it has to offer.

The spotlight plays tricks with the mind.
Encouraging us to be its dirty mistress.
Tip-toeing our way around the rules of the stage.
Leaving those that cannot find it within themselves to participate in the shadows.
Unable to find it within themselves to fight for their rightful place.
Maybe someone else in their life needed it more.
Or they were born without natural stage abilities.
Could it be they were outshined by another?
Or denied their right to the stage?
No matter the reason, they deserve their rightful time in the spotlight.
Unfortunately, with every set of auditions, a lead role must be filled.

Happiness.
What does it look like to you?
Are we told it should look a certain way?
And if so, how do we find it?
How will we know when we have reached it?
Or is happiness just a word we created to reassure ourselves of its existence?
While some people give up on the idea, becoming reckless in their ways, others search their entire life for something they may never find.
A concept few will ever be able to understand.
Money cannot buy you joy.
Possessions do not fill the emptiness within.
Technology cannot be the sole means of seeking out true relationships.
Meaningless sex will not always give you pleasure.
Love is going to hurt just as much as it is going to heal.
Family will let us down every once in a while.
Dreams are going to be crushed.
Life is not always going to be fair.
It is going to be unpredictable.
Happiness, and I mean true happiness, can only exist when we stop looking for it.
We cannot search for something that never wanted to be found in the first place.
It has to find us.

We are constantly signing our lives away.
We drown ourselves in paperwork day in and day out.
Signing paper after paper.
Signing to ensure we are aware of the risks.
Signing to confirm we trust another individual to watch over us.
Signing to guarantee we will come through with our promise.
We go through life coming to accept that we are controlled by our signature.
Something so simple yet so powerful.
With the picking up of a pen, our lives become defined by a contract.
We cannot risk the chance of being unprotected.
Unable to trust someone's truth will remain truthful.
Although these contracts are in our favour,
it's sad to think that we have reached this point in humanity.
The point in time defined by backups, insurance plans, just in cases.
Are we that afraid of failure?
Have we ever considered that exposure to the risk
may be the push we need to truly live?

Welcome everyone to your forty-five minute hot hatha practice.
My name is Society, and I will be your instructor for today's class.
Take these first few minutes to fill the space on your mat.
turns head side to side to see how others are positioned
Connecting with each breath as it enters and exits your lungs.
Okay, focus on the breath, focus on the breath… stop thinking.
Feeling every inhale and exhale as it migrates through your chest.
inha--exhal--inhale---exh---inha--exhal---inhale----exhale----inhale--
As you feel ready, slowly transition onto all fours.
Damn, I was just getting comfy. I guess I'll get up; it'll be good for me.
Then make your way to downward dog, raising hips toward the sky.
Paddle out your feet, stretching the hamstrings to prepare for our first flow.
hesitates
Pretty sure I pulled that the other day. Everyone else is doing it, so screw it, I will too.
All right, let's work our way through this first flow together.
(While our yoga class continues, can I interest you in a lesson of our own?
A course on the dos and don'ts of going with the flow.
A choice to walk in the footsteps of society and its followers,
or to create a path suited toward your individual needs.
A challenge that occurs on your own terms, in your own time.
Keeping this in mind,
I would now like to turn your attention back to the main attraction.)
As we make our way onto our backs for final shavasana,
begin to reconnect with the breath.
gasping for breath, sweat dripping relentlessly down your back
First and last hot yoga class for me.
glances at self in the mirror
Wow, I look disgusting.
looks at the rest of the class
How do people make this look so effortless?
Use this time to reflect on the time spent on your mat.
the breath finally starts to settle
Next yoga class I need to set my own pace.
Namaste.
listens to everyone as they repeat back namaste
Next time the flow of movement will be determined by me.

Before I had the pleasure of meeting creativity, I lived life by the rules.
I drew between the lines.
I saw failure as a dead end.
I blindly followed the facts.
I limited myself to what others told me to be true.
When I embraced my ability to create, I became my own legislator.
I scribbled vigorously through colouring books.
I freed myself from the restraints of knowledge.
I was given the opportunity to find my own truth.
Creativity means something different to every individual.
Whether that is brushing paint on a fresh canvas,
developing a new project for work,
or bringing a child into this world.
Whatever it is you choose to create,
create it with all you've got.
Create when others turn away.
Create what makes you feel real.
Create with no expectations.
Create simply because you can.

Everyone seems to be waiting for their next break.
The next chance they have to take time away from their regular life.
To get away from it all.
To splurge on the next big vacation.
We are constantly wishing away time from our daily routine.
Wishing it away until the time we wanted off so desperately has passed.
We build up to these moments that come and go.
What happened to enjoying each and every day as it comes?
Everyone wishes they could reach a future date,
yet the day you are presently in was once your future.
Yesterday you saw today as a chance to be better.
To make something of yourself.
Although the future holds hope,
we are becoming a world that has lost hope in the present.
The time we have on earth should not be wasted wishing time away.
One day we are here, and the next we are not.
You never know when your last day will come.
Age is just a number.
Tomorrow is just another day.
Fear is just an allusion.
You are just another star in the sky.
Don't let age define your limits.
Make today your day.
Laugh in fear's face.
Let your star shine so brightly that the moon will be jealous.

I constantly seek out adventure.
Travelling the world gives you the opportunity to meet new people.
To see new things.
To open your eyes to the possibilities.
For some, this may be the discovery of a secret closet in their house.
For others, it is an ancient sculpture halfway across the world.
The potential is endless.
Takes lifetimes to experience.
Grasp on to as much of it as you can.
Life is too short to fear the unknown.
Feel the fear and do it anyway.
Go beyond your regular lifestyle.
Take a deeper look at the world around you.
It is out there just waiting for you to explore.
So go out and do it.

Social media has created a new world.
Feeding off pictures, comments, and ideas.
Fuelled by what lies at the tips of our fingers.
Feeling the need, the obligation, to have full awareness of our devices.
These devices that set out to hypnotize us.
Encouraging us to see past the present to the world of social media.
Transforming us into a screen world.
Although we acknowledge our addiction to this new drug,
can we admit that we wish it ceased to exist?
We consistently miss out on life.
Choosing to, instead, scroll down our feed.
Choosing to vicariously live through others' posts.
Choosing to neglect our own experiences.
That is, until we decide to capture it for our next profile update.
Although I encourage you to share your life with others,
promise me it does not get in the way of living.

No one can hear my old soul calling out for help,
my spirit trapped within my young body,
and the young souls surrounding it.
Although it would never change its ancient ways,
it feels incredibly out of place.
Although it is surrounded by people,
it feels utterly alone.
So it continues to scream.

We have become a world of users.
We take what we want.
We dispose of it when we see fit.
We use alcohol and drugs to numb the pain.
We use lies and power to get further in life.
We use food to fill our empty heart.
We use each other to feel a sense of worth.
We use any and every distraction we can get our hands on.
We know it is wrong, yet we continue to use.
And then there are the used.
Why did they become someone or something that deserved to be owned?
By continuing to use them, we grow further and further from our true selves.
Constantly intoxicating ourselves as a means to answer life's problems.
Selfishness and greed are not the tools needed to reach your goals.
Manipulating others is not the path to growing solid relationships.
Feeding our bellies with food will not change our broken feelings.
We use simply because we can, not because we need to.

Judgement.
The ability to create one's own conclusion.
Allowing yourself to believe you know why people are the way they are.
Building a story based on the knowledge you think you "possess."
The key word in that sentence is "think."
You think you know them.
Judging a story you didn't read.
Maybe you glanced over it, flipping through a page or two.
You thought you could read between the lines.
You grasped the information you deemed necessary and left the rest.
Judging someone for who they are
or what they have done is not your responsibility.
People do things for a million reasons.
If that person wishes to share that, they may.
But if they don't, it is not your place to fill in the blanks.
Judging another for their wrongdoings is unfair.
We all have wrongs.
No matter the size,
they are actions we participated in.
Judgement is for those that do not possess the power to accept their own wrongs.
Instead, they hide behind others' weaknesses.
Having an opinion on the matter is acceptable,
as long as you are aware of the ways in which you present it.
What are your intentions?
Are you simply participating as a means to exploit them?
Will this action hurt them, or open them to new ways of thinking?
At the end of the day, is it really worth it?
Let them live their lives while you live yours.
Be kind.
Accept others for who they are.
Choose to be good, and others will follow.

Gentlemen are a scarce breed.
Finding one is a miracle,
so hold on tight if you are lucky enough to find one.
Hold on to them as if they were a unicorn.
Hold on to the type of man that opens the car door for you.
The type of man that tells you that you are beautiful.
The type of man that actually listens to you.
The type of man that sacrifices for you.
The type of man worth waiting for.
In today's society, the term "gentleman" has been downgraded.
Stripped to its core.
Remember the true definition of a gentleman and settle for nothing less.
As for boys,
don't forget to strive to be one.

Find someone to accompany you in silence.
Fearless of the discomfort associated with reaching such a state.
Instead, choosing to fill it with meaningless conversation.
Using it as a means to avoid being awkward.
Unable to be inferior to the silence.
Failing to see the abundance of noise this world holds.
The type of noise that silences silence itself.
Living day to day unable to see the truth in the presence of silence.
If you can find just one person that finds comfort in nothing but silence, hold on to them.
Learn from them.
Grow from them.
Share the silence when words are not needed.

Why do we think less of certain people?
How did they not deserve a second chance?
What gave us the right to have power over them?
Who decided to label the group over the individual?
Labelling them for their actions and mistakes.
Their religious belief.
Their skin colour.
Their sexual identity.
Born into a world that hated them before they could speak their first word.
Born a victim to their environment.
Born with a few more hoops to go through than the rest.
Urging them on to jump through life like a never-ending obstacle course.
Historically, the superior population of white males would be guilty of all charges,
but it is important to remember that they too were born into a specific role.
Not to say some did not take advantage of said positions,
but they merely adapted to their surroundings.
Or at least their depiction of adaptation,
no matter how sick or twisted it may have been.
Unfortunately, these stereotypes tend to get the best of us.
If you wear a hijab, you are probably a terrorist.
If you are homeless, you are most likely going to spend my spare change on drugs.
If you wear tuxedoes and drive a Mercedes, you are going to be a prick.
Although these judgements are harsh and offensive,
you are lying to me if they have never crossed your mind.
What if the person wearing the hijab were seeking refuge,
escaping from the one place they could call home?
What if that homeless individual lost everything at once,
starting with their job and ending with a notice on their doorstep?
What if that wealthy man came from nothing,
having no one to thank for his success except himself?
Never let the group justify the individual.
Give people a chance to be who they are,
not what the world tells them to be.

Trees are unappreciated.
Inhaling our unwanted carbon dioxide.
Exhaling the very oxygen we need to survive.
Sheltering and furnishing our homes.
Creating mesmerizing fires to warm those surrounding it.
Providing food and medicine to nourish its fellow creatures.
Colouring the world with a sea of lush green.
Never failing to give us what we need.
And for what?
How do we show our gratitude to these trees?
Oh right, we cut another one down.
We keep cutting and cutting until there are no more trees to cut.
Although I realize these beings are a necessary resource,
have we not overcompensated our need for them just a touch?
How many decorative chairs,
one-time-use Christmas trees,
and overly tall fences do we need?
Are we really doing the humble tree justice?
Have we ever thought about the tree?
The possibility that they might have something to say?
How can we decide that their life is not worth considering?

It fits ever so tightly in the grasp of your hand.
A piece of equipment you refuse to disconnect from.
This thing that manipulates you to believe your very survival depends on it.
An object that gives you the courage to say whatever you please.
The screen acting as a barricade from reality.
Enabling you to think there are no consequences.
That is, until that username you so quickly called out
transforms into a living and breathing person.
Standing in front of you,
wondering what they did to deserve this.
Unable to comprehend you were simply doing as society taught you.

Fake people.
Fact or myth?
Fact: this term is used beyond its boundaries.
Myth: this word is an appropriate identifier.
Truth: everyone hides behind the person they want to be,
not the person they are.
No matter how cruel, plastic, or perfect someone is, they are real.
No matter how easy it may be to say someone is fake, it is not fair.
People cannot be measured by how much makeup they wear.
The number of followers they have on Instagram.
The crowd they associate with.
The possessions they choose to fashion or display.
Because, at the end of the day, a person is just a person.

Perspective.
Although we all want to be Mr. or Mrs. Right,
there is always more than one right answer to any given problem.
Your perspective has many variables,
dependant on where you come from.
What you have witnessed.
The experiences you have faced.
An equation that forges a never-ending array of perspectives.
Therefore, no one person can change or redefine another's belief.
Instead, use this mathematic formula as an opportunity to learn.
To see the world from their point of view.
When given the choice, please don't judge a book by its cover.
Let people be who they were built to be.
Acknowledge that everyone will have an opinion.
Respect their values.
And if you can't... smile, nod, and walk away.
We are meant to be different from each other.
We are meant to be unique.
We are meant to have perspective.

Connections give us a sense of belonging.
It's about the little moments you share with others.
These moments are what get us through the day.
Make it worth getting up every morning.
We pretend to be invincible.
Manipulating ourselves to believe we are indestructible.
But we need people.
We need each other.
Connections root us to the ground.
Allowing us to find a sense of securement.
We need it like plants need water.
So think twice before bending the hose to someone's water supply.
Don't let their roots shrivel up.
Leaving them to die along with the rest of them.
Use your words to love, not to hurt.
If you cannot do so, simply don't say anything at all.
Choose to walk away before inflicting harm that you can't take back.
Everyone deserves to belong.
We grow with, not against, each other.

I love you.
Three syllables that show how much you care.
A short, yet powerful, sentence.
Not to be reckoned with.
Then why is it that people say *I love you* as if they were saying "hello"?
Love is so much more than that.
Deserving only to those you sincerely love.
It can take years to nurture.
It does not simply appear out of thin air.
Saying this set of words shows you accept another
for everything that makes up who they are.
We all get to choose who we love.
Whether that is a family member, friend, or life partner.
Take time to get to know a person.
Then you can determine if they are worthy
of these three insanely important words.

We are all background noise.
Background noise to each other's symphony.
Symphonies that long to be heard.
Shouting out in the hope that someone will listen.
Shouts that become engulfed by a dark void.
A void that we, as a people, create.
A void that takes our shouts and turns them into whispers.
Whispers lost in the wind.
Unwanted and forgotten.
We disoriented them.
Stole their sense of direction.
Placed them in a maze without a map to guide them.
In doing so, we knowingly sent them to their doom.
Allowing the void to consume them.
All because we chose to ignore our ability to listen.
Enabling our ears to hear what others have to say.
Not necessarily because we want to be rude.
But because this act of silencing ensures we will be the only one heard.
Yet a symphony is not possible without many musicians.
The abundance of artists that allow a piece to be whole.
We all want to be heard.
What we fail to see is the importance of the power of unity.
We each play our instrument as loud as it can possibly sound.
Yet we still end up feeling this sense of emptiness.
We feel sympathy for the banished whispers.
Because we are those whispers.
And so the void is created.
Find the strength to destroy your part in the void.
Instead, choose to fill it with the symphony of each other.
Building an orchestra of humanity.
By doing so, the void no longer has the power to exist.

Silence is misunderstood.
Humans feel the constant need to fill emptiness.
As a people, we struggle to leave things untouched.
Control overpowers us, thus overpowering the peace.
If a state of absolute rest is achieved, we find a means to disrupt it.
Intentionally doing so, neglecting our ability to remain still.
Fearful we will be trapped within our thoughts.
Or rather not being able to express our thoughts.
A craving to hear our own voice.
A need to entertain our surroundings.
A silent conversation cannot be deemed as a proper interaction.
If so, you have failed as a human being.
You are awkward.
You are weird.
And this is why silence is the enemy.
We fear not being accepted.
By doing so, we have lost our ability to embrace the silence.
To take in the little moments.
To simply be.
Forgetting we need silence.

Imagine a world without money.
A world without greed.
A world without taxes.
A world without bills.
Now imagine a world of sharing.
A world of compassion.
A world of simply working for the better good.
A world of love for one another and not for objects.
Just imagine.

If you have a plate of food on the table, you are lucky.
If you have a roof over your head, you should be overjoyed.
If you have a loving support system, you are blessed.
If you have a decent education, you should be grateful.
We should be appreciative of what we have,
but instead we choose to focus on what we don't have.
While the less fortunate would give anything for just one of the above,
we would give it all up for one shot to make "something" of ourselves.
All they want is a life free from the thought of how their family will eat tonight.
A life that ensures the luxury of safety.
A life with potential to achieve a goal.
While the things we think we need are just things.
Things that we think will make our lives better.
Instead, I challenge you to be countercultural.
Be happy for the life you have been given.
Be something more than this materialistic society.
Be the person you want to be.
Whatever it is you are going to be, be it with all you've got.
Use the resources you have been given.
Be thankful for what you have, when so many are not.

People never fail to find a reason to be mad at the world.
Mad at what it has become.
Mad at those inhabiting it.
Pointing their fingers at anything except themselves.
Whether it's politicians, the youth, or even the weather,
there is always someone else to blame for their miseries.
High school is a great example of this never-ending cycle of blame.
Parents blame other children for the suffering of their child.
Teachers blame cellphones for their students' lack of interest in their education.
Teenagers blame each other for the continuous drama and bully-like behaviours.
What if parents simply talked to their child
instead of blaming other adolescents?
What if teachers addressed their issues with the tech savvy generation
instead of blaming students for the society they were born into?
What if teenagers were unbiased and chose to spread kindness
instead of blaming their peers for a situation they all contribute to?
The moment a change in mindset occurs, a ripple effect will inevitably follow.
Initiate change wherever and whenever you can.
Help the victims, because we are all victims of something.
Victims of crime or emotional setbacks or hunger or bullying.
We are also all perpetrators,
whether by laughing at a harmful remark or beating someone in a back alley.
If you cannot recall such a time, you are only lying to yourself.
The cycle is constant and exists because we all allow it to.
It's a constant cycle of being hurt and hurting.
A cycle of blaming each other for the pain we created.
Did you notice the part in that sentence that mentioned "we"?
We are all to blame.
The first human being to walk this Earth would have experienced peace,
but then came pain.
And with that pain came anger.
Anger that led to revenge.
Revenge that led to pain being inflicted on yet another person.
Next time you feel yourself drawn toward this cycle,
choose to forgive those who have harmed you.
Break the cycle of blame.
Start the cycle of love.

STAR LIGHT, STAR BRIGHT

Out of all of the possible people that could have existed, you are here.
Generations upon generations of ancestors
helped in the formation of the unique being that makes up you.
If one of these many people had not met their partner, you would cease to exist.
A mom or dad or distant grandparent left unborn.
Completely rearranging your fate.
Yet by some miracle your parents met each other.
Creating the specific set of genes that make up who you are.
You are here against all odds.
You are here when it easily could have been someone else.
Someone else's soul that set out in search of a body and never found one.
Where is it that these souls find life, if it is not through life itself?
I have this theory that these beings are what form a star.
Acting as a reminder of the beautiful opportunity we have been given.
Watching over us for all of eternity.
Sending a beacon of hope.
Encouraging us to live on for them when there is nothing left to live for.
Live on for those that never got the chance to live.
Live on for the lonely souls that pierce light through the darkness.
Live on, because life is worth living.

"Batter, batter, batter, swing," taunts the other team as you attempt to focus.
"And another foul ball," declares the announcer through diamond speakers.
"Strike one, strike two, strike three, you're out," shouts the umpire.
Time to call your own defeat
as you regretfully make your way back to the bench.
Awaiting your shot at redemption in outfield.
A means to defend your honour.
One inning in,
an infinite amount of potential left to be had.
Nine rounds alternating offence and defence.
Baseball.
The game of softballs and bats.
The sport of sold out stadiums and beers.
The field of lost hopes and dreams.
A metaphor in the making for mental health.

Rate your pain from zero to ten.
Zero being no pain.
Ten being the worst pain you have ever felt.
Are there any provoking factors?
What is the quality of the pain?
Where does it radiate from?
How severe is it?
Is it worse in certain situations?
What is your understanding of it?
Healthcare providers pose this set of questions to their patients on a daily basis.
The tricky part is that pain is incomparable.
No one person's experience of pain will be identical to that of another.
Whether it is physical or otherwise.
Pain is individual.
Undefinable by anyone except its host.
Someone's worst nightmare may be another's dream come true.
This does not mean the first person's suffering
should no longer be considered valid.

I am a numbers person.
Numbers on the scale.
The number of pounds I want to see reflecting back at me.
The number of centimetres my waist measurements could be.
The number of calories I need to restrict in order to get results.
The number of minutes I work out a day to effectively reproportion myself.
The problem with numbers is they are never-ending.
Counting on to eternity.
As do I,
as I count out the number of things I wish I could change about my body.

There's pain behind her blue eyes.
Blue is a tricky colour, because it represents so many things.
It represents sadness and suffering, a case of the blues.
Blue represents the blue stretches of water
that give everyone and everything life.
It represents the bright blue skies that watch over us
before turning to the moon for the night shift.
Blue comes in many shades, each with their own emotion.
But her eyes are dark blue.
The type of blue that runs deep with mystery.
The type of blue you find on the floor of the ocean.
The type of blue few can understand.
Her eyes hold so much beauty,
but little do people know they are hurting.
Hurting because they have seen life put to shame.
Hurting because they want to close their eyelids
to take a break from what they are witnessing.
Hurting because no one else has the courage to take
a long stare into her eyes to see both the pain and the joy.
Maybe the blue in her eyes is undefinable.
Not the sad type of blue or the life giving type of blue.
Maybe they are just blue.

It goes unseen by others,
yet felt and understood by all.
The battle against ourselves.
The battle from within.
The battle of self rejection.
A locked door to which we all possess the key.
Neglecting to use it.
Little do we know this tiny object holds our potential.
Waiting ever so patiently to be unleashed.
Opening the door to unite body with mind
rather than suppressing the mind from what it truly is.
Allowing the body to deceive its surroundings as a means to blend in,
similar to a chameleon.
Adapting to the outside world in the hope that its insides will remain intact.
Unlike a chameleon,
the predators we face are a figment of our imagination.
Ironically, the only predator we face is our imagination.
Imagining time and time again what others would think of our true colours.

I'm waiting.
Waiting for everything to fall apart.
I'm coming.
Coming to understand what people mean by "it's too good to be true."
I'm questioning.
Questioning why so much good brings me to such a dark place.

You are my sunshine,
my only sunshine.
You make me happy when skies are grey.
You'll never know, dear,
how much I love you.
Please don't take my sunshine away.
But they took me.
I took myself.
Allowing them to drain my light.
Sucking the life force out of me.
Taking and taking and taking.
Taking until there was nothing left to take.
Taking until I was no longer your sunshine.

When you lose weight,
do not lose yourself in the process.
It is a game of snakes and ladders.
A board, two dice, four playing pieces, multiple opponents.
One objective: make it to the top.
Cleanse, diet, fast, restrict, slim out, starve.
Walk, bike, run, hit the gym, hit it twice.
Burn, baby, burn.
Burn until there's nothing left.
Burn before all you have left do to is come sliding down.
Leaving the dice to gamble with your health: mental and physical.
Each pawn on the board game representing a piece of you.
Player red: the mind.
Stuck at start, awaiting its turn.
Player blue: the body.
Hitting the jackpot as it climbs the first ladder.
Player green: the mirror.
Landing on the snake's head; taking the first fall.
Player yellow: the spectator.
Following behind, attempting to keep up with the rest.

A smile holds secrets.
Physically stealing the body of its right to speak.
Leaving our voice behind.
Behind a false gesture of happiness.
Behind a set of white teeth.
Behind an unwilling smile.
The lips play a role the rest of our body cannot.
Putting on a production for the eyes of the outside world.
Acting in the hope that one day that smile will become a reality.

It is scary how little people actually know about the true me.
It is difficult to fully open up in this world.
It is saddening to realize how sheltered we all are.
How alone I feel standing in a crowd.
How isolated you allow your body to become.
How little we seem to recognize others in the same predicament.
It takes one second to initiate change.
One smile to let someone know they are acknowledged.
One conversation to let an individual know they are heard.
One moment of impact that saves a life.

"Let's play a game," you shout to me as you motion toward the pool.
"We will take turns saying a phrase under water," you explain.
"Once I have completed the sentence," you continue,
"we will meet at the water's surface, and you will guess what I just said."
I have to admit, at first this underwater pastime has its perks.
In my efforts to read your lips, to learn the tongue of the mermaids,
I fall for the childlike wonder we find in our ability to recreate the spoken word.
But as time goes on, I outgrow the game.
Pulling at your arms, pleading you to resurface
so that I might be able to hear your voice clearly once again.
But your unwilling strength outwits mine.
I inhale, diving one last time into the depths of the pool to meet you.
Screaming through the water in the hopes that you will listen to me.
My words are left with no choice but to accompany the bubbles
as they make their journey to the world above.
Escaping the need to be heard by you.
Allowing your ears to fill with water particles.
Acting as earplugs to the voices you cannot bring yourself to hear.
Accepting this defeat,
I push the souls of my feet on the vinyl liner of the pool.
Choosing to soak up the sunshine.
Holding the towel beside me.
Holding it with the intention that you will join me when you are ready.
Holding on to the person I know you to be above and below the water's surface.

People pick and choose what others get to see.
We laugh away our sadness.
We engage in small talk to hide our depth.
We make up white lies to conceal big truths.
We are all constantly hiding, but from what?
We all continue to push our true selves farther and farther from the surface,
until the surface forms into a person we no longer recognize.
Why is it that we chose to bury the real us beneath this person in the first place?
Do we fear what others will think of the true us?
Will we crush our soul if we expose it to the outside world?
Can the world accept what we have to offer?
We are all born as a single individual
with one interconnected mind, body, and spirit.
Don't dig a grave within yourself to bury your spirit.

Sometimes people contemplate pulling trig,
while others count down the days until they can pull the trigger.
Whether it is a finger, gun, or otherwise,
we all have vices.
A means to put to rest the devil on our shoulder.
The devil that comes in many forms.
The devil that never sleeps.
The sneaky little bastard that always finds a way back to us
from the trenches of hell.
No matter how deep the grave,
he will crawl relentlessly until reaching the ground's surface.
No matter how many times he is strangled,
his suffocated blue face will return, red once more.
No matter how convinced we may be that his heart has stopped beating,
he finds a means to resuscitate himself.
There is only one way to escape from his clutches.
Prove to him that he no longer has power over you.
Banish the weapons he whispered for you to use.
Throw them into the belly of the ocean
where no one but the sea creatures can find them.
Take control of the life that was always yours and never his.

Taking time to think is a very important activity in everyone's life.
It allows us to analyze difficult situations.
To remember magical moments.
To understand why certain actions were taken.
To help rebuild ourselves.
To see the beauty in life as we reflect on the past, present, and future.
To appreciate anything and everything we have encountered.
When we are angry,
it allows us to take a step back from the argument to see both sides of the story.
When we are happy,
it allows us to constantly take pictures in our mind of the greatness occurring.
When we are sad,
it tells us to push forward, because we have so much happiness to live for.
It is healthy to evaluate life's experiences,
as long as you do not allow them to overpower you.
Do not overthink to the point of insanity.
To the point that leads you to replay a situation over and over in your head.
A situation you wish you could change but no longer can.
Think clearly and with meaning.
Think far and wide and outside of the box.
Think deeply and with compassion.
Never lose yourself in the interconnected web that makes up your mind.
Instead, grow the web like a delicate spider would,
so that it will become complex and strong.

My body.
A constant fight with cellulite.
Too much curve versus too little.
The double chin that appears when I laugh.
Fat that collects in my lower abdomen.
Irregularly chubby fingers.
A head that out grew the rest of me.
A list of my insecurities in less than a minute.
You may not see them, but my eyes cannot help themselves.
Pinpointing my least favourite qualities every time a mirror is in sight.
Body image is a battle of mind and matter.
The mind: what we want our body to look like.
The matter: what our body actually looks like.
An unreachable state of coexistence between the two.
However, battles can be won.
And with each day, I face a new one.
Today I feel victorious.
Tomorrow I might take a loss.
And the day after that I'll continue the fight.
The fight to love my body.

I choose me.
I choose to be the best Alexandria I can be.
I choose my needs over those of the needy people.
I choose a life lived cohesively with happiness.
I choose where I go from here.
I choose self love.
But it's easier said than done.
So I'll take it one step at a time.
First, eliminate the negativity.
Stop letting evil call the shots.
Cut out the people, tasks, places, things, et cetera
that make you feel less than worthy.
Second, indulge in the things you love most.
Make them a priority.
Incorporate them into your everyday routine.
Third, keep it real.
Don't change for anybody.
Stay true to who you know yourself to be.
Choose you.

Time allows us to heal.
At first, the pain is excruciating and unimaginably difficult.
But as time goes on, our wounds slowly begin to heal and eventually fade away.
Sometimes it scars, acting as a reminder of the challenging experiences
that shaped us into the person we are today.
A reminder of past mistakes,
moments of weakness,
the darkest parts of ourselves.
It's important not to be ashamed of our scars,
because they are beautiful and make up a significant part of who we are.
Even a vibrant rose has its thorns.
That does not mean it is not rare and abundant with life.
The real people in your life will love you for the good and bad,
the light and darkness,
the happiness and suffering.
Love who you are, and use your scars to grow into a better you.
The type of you that you can be truly proud of.
Everyone deserves to be loved and to love themselves.
Do not let the dark moments cast a shadow over the amazing light
each and every one of us shines out to the world.

When no one's watching, we are our true selves.
We are able to express all of our parts.
The parts that no one else gets to see.
When no one's watching, I don't need a mirror to critique myself.
I am pure, because no one has the ability to judge me for my scars.
When no one's watching me, I can dance.
Not just the hopping up and down kind of dance,
but the earth shaking kind of dance.
When no one's watching, I let my feelings unleash.
I can become whoever I want to be,
whether it's an emotional wreck lying on the floor,
or an overly joyful person with an idiotic smile on my face.
When no one's watching,
I pretend I'm the only person that exists on this planet,
sometimes even the whole universe.
When no one's watching, I get to be me.
Because who else is there to be if not me?

It's hard to believe how high I built my wall.
Stuck in the silence and harshness of those you told yourself you were close to.
A cycle of never-ending lies, ridicule, and constant confusion.
So the wall continued to grow and grow and grow until I trapped myself,
making it impossible to be reached by others.
The funny thing is when you build a wall, you lose sight of everyone else.
You are not tall enough to see over your own wall.
You can't see that there are others who have built similar walls.
Knocking down these walls is a terrifying, yet rewarding, moment.
That moment you finally expose yourself to the outside world.
I have come to realize that it is not about hiding
from the things that kept you down for so long.
It is about seeing past them.

Self appreciation.
I love you.
And by you, I mean me.
I love me.
How often do you sit down with yourself?
Glance in the mirror.
Make time for me time.
How often do you accompany these actions with a moment of self gratitude?
A minute.
A second.
A space in time to celebrate who you are.
Inside and out.

I am strong.
I don't want to say it out loud, not even to myself sometimes.
But I am mighty.
I may not always want to take the high road, but I know I will.
I would say I am pretty tough.
Not everything is going to work out exactly how I want it to,
so I take on the curveballs as they come.
This leads me to believe I am resilient.
I know my truths and choose to share them with the world.
One might say I am courageous.
I urge every bone and muscle in my body
to face the demons that come sprinting toward me,
no matter how much I may want to turn and run in the opposite direction.
And by doing so, I am brave.
Take time to recognize that you are significantly strong.
It may not always be a physical strength, or maybe it is.
The point is, no matter what it may be, we are all strong in one way or another.
Although we may not always feel we are mighty or tough
or resilient or courageous or even brave,
we deserve acknowledgement for our strength each and every day.
Give yourself a pat on the back, because life isn't always picture perfect,
no matter how much we may convince ourselves to believe so.
You made it through another day.
If that is not strength, then I don't know what is.

EXCEPTIONALLY ORDINARY

A camera lens out of focus.
A grouping of words without meaning.
An action without purpose.
A lion lacking its roar.
Life is not always about following a straight path.
Sometimes we need to expose ourselves to the mind's potential.
Expose it to the unrealistic trains of thought.
Expose it to the creativity trapped within each and every one of us.
Expose it to the unknown mysteries of life.
Take time to focus on the unfocused.

Do you ever get stuck?
Stuck on a feeling, emotion, or mindset.
Losing yourself in the passion of the experience.
Reality miles away.
No intent in your mind of reaching it.
Allowing you to see life at a view that will forever take your breath away.
A life your eyes wish to remain eternally stuck on.
Not the type of stuck that leaves sticky glue all over your hands.
Or the type of stuck that chains you down unwillingly.
Rather, the type of stuck that numbs you to the core.
Numbs you as a means to keep you in that moment.
The moment you finally feel a sense of life.
Not just a breathing person with a heartbeat.
A person that has fallen in love with life.

You hear the water calling you.
You see it slowly dragging back toward the sea.
You feel the ocean trickling between your toes.
The energy recollecting for the next wave.
Grasping on to every droplet of water.
As fast as the water meets your feet, it creeps away.
Sprinting across the sand with purpose.
The calm blue transforms into a sheet of white.
Releasing the power of the ocean as the waves come crashing down.
It's the beautiful simplicities in life, like this, that leave me speechless.
A feeling rooted deep within me.
A warmth that radiates out to the universe.
A love for the opportunities given to me.
A need to discover as many of these life-altering experiences as I can.

1 day.
24 hours.
1440 minutes.
86 400 seconds.
With each new day, a new opportunity is born.
The sun's rise until its set brings with it infinite potential.
Never let yesterday define your today.
There's no better time than the present.
If today does not turn out as you envisioned,
sleep it off, knowing tomorrow is another day.

Every person has a place where they feel at peace.
A home away from home.
My place of tranquility is a path that runs along my local forest.
The trees canopy above me, forming a safety net.
The end of its long stretch reveals a shining light.
Creating a mysterious tunnel that leads its travellers to a beautiful opening.
As I walk under the pine, I feel a sense of protection from the outside world.
A means to escape reality.
Inhaling the exhale of the forest.

Lose yourself in another's imagination.
Absorbing the art displayed by others.
The art of the written word.
Inviting us to enter the world of creativity.
Hours on end in another dimension.
Buried in the pages of a novel.
Walking in the footsteps of the characters.
Learning from their path.
A path painted by the colourful pictures of the mind.
Heroes rising to defeat the evil ways of a villain.
Pirates setting out to sea in search of hidden treasure.
Killers hunted down by a team of investigators.
Plots run endless.
Feeding your eyes with a story.
Feeding your mind with knowledge.
Feeding your heart with the passion forged to create.

You turn the volume as high as the speakers allow.
Windows gliding all the way down.
Inviting the breeze from all directions.
Causing your hair to dance in the wind.
Sunlight trickling through the trees.
Playing a game of hide and go seek.
Autumn leaves colour the road ahead.
Forming a tunnel of overhanging branches.
The song blaring from the radio concludes as you reach the stop sign.
As your foot lifts from the brakes, car accelerating, a beat starts.
Speeding up in unison with the vehicle.
Pulsating through your body.
The road twists and bends.
Pleading for you to dance with it.
Encouraging your free spirit to life.
Eyes lost in the stretches of land around you.
Calling you to walk freely in the fields.
Overpowered by the notes that flow out of your car speaker.
Urging you back to reality as you pull into the driveway.

A place, object, time, individual.
A small town duck pond.
A worn out stuffed buffalo.
A clock displaying 11:11a.m.
A mother and son registering for a run.
For some, these things are nothing more than a noun.
For others, their world is defined by them.
Revealing the deepest parts of yourself.
The trigger ignited from their presence.
Impossible to express in words.
It is better this way.
A secret kept as your own.
Left unsaid because no one can understand it better than you.

The determining factors of our life.
Moments that shape an individual.
Coincidences that are not so coincidental at all.
Events that impact the person we were, are, and become.
Who knew a childhood of stuttering would lead to a humbling confidence.
Who knew a “help wanted” sign would bring so many significant people my way.
Who knew a rare blood vessel disease would ignite my passion to care for others.
Who knew a text message would guide me to a prospering independence.
Who knew a notebook from Chapters would become filled with my writing.
Who knew a half marathon running event would bring me to you.
Who knew a few minuscule events would determine the person I am today.

Home.
A rather generic term.
Associated with the four walls that support a house.
A stack of bricks.
A piecing together of wood.
A block of molded clay.
Yet a home means so much more.
A comfort zone.
A place to escape the outside world.
A refuge where we can be ourselves.
Not to be defined by shape, colour, size, or model.
But instead by the memories formed with the ones we love.
A gut feeling that calls us home.
The house may change, but never the home.
A home is shared in the hearts of the people you choose to invite in.

A true friend is like your favourite shirt.
The comfy, worn-out one you can always find lying around.
Never letting you down when you need it most.
Well, that is, unless it is stashed away in the laundry bin once again.
Mine is a blue and red flannel.
I wear it anywhere and everywhere.
Wrapped around my waist on a night out.
Complementing a tank top for a hike.
Buttoned up for a long day of work at the farm.
As a pajama shirt on cold winter nights.
No matter the occasion, I can always count on it.
Unlike a tube top or sweatpants or ripped jeans,
the shirt never fails to find purpose.
Sometimes the shirt goes missing.
Buried in the wardrobe or temporarily stolen by my little sister.
No matter the reason for its absence,
it will always find a way back into my life.
The shirt will be my friend,
forever and always.

The resonating smell of fire.
It's the smell of camping weekends with my cousins.
The smell of winter days spent reading by the fire.
The smell of pie irons and s'mores with my mom, dad, and sister.
The smell of shared drinks and laughter amongst friends.
The smell of the coals that accompany me as I admire the stars.
The smell of the places in time I feel at home.
Thank you fire, for making my hair smell the following morning.
Thank you fire, for leaving your imprint on my favourite baseball cap.
Thank you fire,
for giving me the opportunity to create memories I will never forget.

Unimaginably perfect.
Unplanned and oh so sweet.
Creating a tingling sensation that runs through your entire body.
The ability to let yourself go.
A night drive screaming out your favourite songs with friends.
The embrace of a warm hug from a missed loved one.
That moment you realize you have finally achieved your goals.
Leaving you profoundly free.
Disconnecting you from the world.
Feeding your soul as would a beautiful sunset that feeds your eyes.
Cleansing your body like the ocean's salty water that purifies your skin.
Shining light into your life similar to the stars that brighten the night sky.

Compassion.
Love.
Kindness.
A simple hello.
Initiating a conversation.
Offering a smile.
Simple actions.
Actions that serve to save lives.
So I ask you, when given the opportunity,
to love the unloved.
Give without expecting in return.
Stand up for those suffering.
Be someone for somebody.
Shine a light in the darkness.
Live for those around you.

Hug the headphones around your ears.
Slide the auxiliary cable in place.
Scroll through your playlists.
Select one that suits your mood.
Hit shuffle.
Music on, world off.
Giving complete power to the predesignated DJ.
Each beat working effortlessly to pulsate through your body.
From the sappy love stories of country to the rebellious ways of rock and roll.
Influencing each listener differently.
An individual song heard from a million perspectives.
Appealing to the senses in the form of sound.
A free therapy for all that subscribe.
The guardian angel that is music.

From idea to reality.
Check list to check mark.
A single dollar bill to millions.
Humans are task oriented beings.
Constantly on the go.
Driven by their success.
Failing to see beauty in little things.
Feeding on the need to reach a set goal.
Ensuring their moment in the spotlight.
An objective serving to justify our existence.
What if, instead, we existed for today?
What if we took a minute to be one with the world around us?
What if we lived to admire the simplicity of it all?

I hope you are lucky enough to have a rock in your life.
That one person you can always count on.
That one person you feel completely yourself around.
They see the worst and best in you.
A parent, sibling, friend, mentor, or spouse.
Always there with an ear to listen.
A joke to make you laugh.
A shoulder for you to cry on.
A word of advice to evoke thought.
A place for you to be at peace.
A person you cannot go without.
Hold on to your rock.
Show your appreciation.
Love them for the person they are for you.
Love them even when you hate them.
Love them because they rock your world.

Live life with meaning.
We only get one lifetime to reach our maximum potential.
One chance to make something of ourselves.
One opportunity to initiate change.
Do not waste your time doing anything less.
Every minute counts.
Say hi to your neighbour.
Be nice to the outsiders.
Embarrass yourself every once in a while.
See every challenge as an opportunity to learn.
Leave the drama behind.
Tell those close to you that you love them.
Take time to live a little.
Isn't that why we are all here?

The universe speaks to us.
Sends us a beacon of hope.
Humours us to change.
Guides us when we are lost.
Encourages us to look up.
Nudges us in the right direction.
Gives us a sign.
My great-grandmother lived in the big city once upon a time.
There she met the love of her life,
my great-grandfather.
They decided to leave the city and raise their family in a small town.
Years later, after the passing of her husband,
she moved back to the city where they met.
On move-in day, as she pulled up to her apartment,
she noticed something strangely familiar about the street name.
It was Fredrick Street, my great-grandfather's name.
Although they were not physically together just maybe
the universe wanted her to know that he was with her in spirit.

Extraordinary.
Google defines it as something *very unusual or remarkable*.
When you break down the word further,
you are left with "extra" and "ordinary."
Extra ordinary.
I have come to the conclusion that extraordinary things
are not as unusual as we make them out to be.
Rather, they are made up of ordinary things.
Undefinably extra ordinary things.
Sharing a family meal on a weekday.
Curling up to read a good book.
Laughing around a fire with friends.
Waking up beside the one you love.
Now that is extraordinary.
Take time to find extraordinary in the ordinary.

LOST IN LOVE

Years of unforgiveable winters left my heart to freeze over.
Slowly transforming me into a lonely Ice Queen.
Falling for the same pattern with each first snowflake
as it touches down on the blanket of green grass.
Falling for the autumn colours that danced so
effortlessly from the branches of maple trees.
Falling for the fresh start I foolishly saw
in the untouched canvas of white snow.

You stand in a crowd, but I only see you.
You, with this way about you I can't quite describe.
I always see you with the same group, but you are your own person.
You are unlike any of the others, and I want to share that with you.
It's about the way you move and express yourself to others.
No one can see how magnificent you truly are, not even you.
By doing so, you remain under the radar.
We see each other on the occasional night from a distance.
The lights dimmed, the energy of the night pulsating through us.
But I want to know you when the night starts to fade away
and only the moon-gazers remain.
I want to know you like the sun knows the moon.
I need to find a way to you.
Just maybe, if the stars align in the proper formation, they could lead me to you.
Just maybe, as the crowd starts to fade away, you'll look at me.
Just maybe, we can become more than two people
standing on opposite sides of a crowded room.

I fear not finding you.
The person I spend the rest of my life with.
Whoever you may be, I sure as hell hope you are out there.
I hope you will be overjoyed to raise our children.
I hope you will love me as unconditionally as I love you.
I hope we will build a family.
I hope we will grow old together.
I hope to see you sometime soon,
but until then I wait impatiently for you to appear.
Don't let me give up on you.
Don't let my worst fears consume me.
Instead, fill my life with meaning.
Fill my life with you.

This person wants to be a part of my life,
and I think I want them too.
There is this force pulling us together.
Yet I feel this urge from within to run.
A resistance that I knew would be there when I least wanted it.
A deep emotion that would one day consume me.
Although I used every ounce of my will to bury it,
it crept its way to the surface.
There was this person once upon a time that I could not have,
someone I still cannot have.
I convinced myself I had moved on,
gave up on the possibilities.
And honestly, I thought I had.
But here they are, yet again, on my mind.
I'm getting caught in the fantasy.
Maybe I owe it to myself to move on.
To accept this amazing opportunity.
Yet as I typed these very words, the muscles in my fingers urged me to stop.
I have this gut feeling that this one choice will make or break me.
Make or break my heart.
Not only because I think this new person may just have the ability to do so.
I might also break it if and when I let go of my past dreams.
My heart sends my brain into panic mode.
Allowing it to lose control.
Slowly, I regain sanity.
I'm beginning to see how pointless this fear is.
It is time to let the past be the past.
To take on this new person with a new ray of hope.

I want to love someone so much it hurts.
I want to wake up every morning with them on my mind.
I've seen it in movies,
heard people talk about it,
but it's hard to imagine.
Two people utterly lost in each other.
I want to scream at the top of my lungs every time I think about it.
Scream out of frustration that I don't have it.
Out of pure excitement that I may have it one day.
No matter the reason,
love is always playing with me.
Sometimes I think it is in sight.
But I quickly realize I was only trying to make love when it wasn't there.
Hurting those I leave behind with all of the fake love.
I did not mean to inflict such harm;
they were just collateral damage.
Who knows?
Maybe one day I will love someone.
But for now, I'll have to sit back and wait.
The only problem is I don't like waiting.
I'd much rather go out and find it now.
Love is kind of a bitch.
It's also kind of beautiful.
And the more and more I think about it, the crazier I get.
So enough with love for now.

I have a story to tell you.
You may remember the person I saw some time ago in a crowd.
The person I wanted to know more than just as a someone,
but as the one.
I saw them again, and this time they saw me too.
We were more than two distant people in a room.
I felt a power greater than that of the night's energy.
This time I felt an electric current connecting us.
A current I never want to disconnect from.
Yet I fear they are oblivious to this spark.
Oblivious because I continue to dance around my feelings.
Unsure how they would react to my expression of interest.
Scared to unleash the possibilities.
I am not used to making the first move.
I don't think they are either.
Maybe we need to be brave together.
Maybe we need to take a leap of faith.
Because I have this need from within.
This need that keeps leading me back to the thought of you.
Then, just like that,
the only person I wanted to be there was by my side.
They wrapped their arm around me, made me feel safe.
A small gesture that meant the world to me.

Do you ever just click with someone?
Conversations are endless.
Sharing similar, yet unique, views.
Developing an automatic comfort in your own skin.
They seem less of a stranger than the people you've known your entire life.
A scarce breed they are.
Appearing at the oddest of times.
But when they do, you automatically feel a deep connection.
The world becomes a little less scary knowing they exist.
Acting as a beacon of hope.
Hope that this life has purpose.
Hope that you are not alone.
Hope that, with them, tomorrow has possibility.
It is crazy to think that a single person can possess such hope.
A single person who gives your life meaning.

I want you to know my deepest secrets.
My insecurities.
My fears.
My demons.
I want you to understand my twisted beauty.
My inspirations.
My story.
My love.
I want you to see me from the view I see you.
Your brokenness.
Your kindness.
Your boldness.
You may think you are not worth being loved,
but you are worth it to me.
I want all of you.
The good and the bad.
The light and the darkness.
But just as quickly as you fell for me,
you picked yourself up and ran in the opposite direction.
You saw the way my eyes looked into yours.
The smile on my face when I lost myself in you.
My fingers tracing over the scars you tried to forget.
And how it scared you.
If only you knew how scared I was to lose you.
Little did I know you were already lost, and there was no way of finding you.

I feel so exposed.
I'm vulnerable around you in a way I've never quite felt.
It's freeing, but also unbelievably scary.
You have the ability to both make me or break me.
And if you break me, I will shatter into a million pieces.
My heart might not be able to take it.
Although it is strong,
when I am with you,
its barricade transforms into a thin sheet of ice.
And I have a funny feeling I might just fall through.
The ice will slowly break beneath me.
Yet I will continue to remain in place.
My body screaming louder and louder as the cracks continue to form.
Urging me to run off the ice.
But my muscles are stiff.
Stiff because they are secretly in love with the thrill of the unknown.
Stiff because they are afraid if they move the slightest bit, the ice will give way.
Stiff because they have unwavering faith that the ice won't break.
But spring is just around the corner.

Rejection stings.
Stings you like a bee.
Words hitting you like a concrete wall.
Choosing to reject you for a reason of their choice.
Whether that entails a lack of understanding.
Others are unaware of what they mean to you.
Or fearful of the risk your love entails.
No matter the reason, it always hurts.
Hurts because after being rejected, you feel a little more alone.
Hurts because you were exposed, regretfully making yourself vulnerable.
Hurts because the hope you saw in them faded away into nothing.

There's always that one person.
That person who comes in and out of your life.
The person you get butterflies thinking about.
They may not even know you exist,
but they mean everything to you.
Reconnecting with them continues to feed your addiction.
You love the idea of being with them.
Despite the fact that they are already taken by someone else.
You always want them,
but can never have them.

I want your arms wrapped around me ever so tightly.
Each finger tracing its way slowly across my body.
To feel your lips pressed up against mine.
Your numbing kiss that made the world stop.
I need to get lost in your eyes.
I'm afraid I might forget what colour they are.
I demand your presence,
but you aren't there when I call you.
You are the only person I want to be here,
yet the one person I cannot have by my side.
What was once there is now gone.

You are my everything, yet you are my nothing.
I fear the day we become strangers.
I want you, but you are blinded by your own foolishness.
Too lost in your own pain.
In the past.
In the person you struggle to become.
In the what ifs you cannot control.
Too lost to find me.
I need to face these facts.
The facts that I know to be true.
But I can't.
Instead, I allow myself to deteriorate from within
while attempting to keep my surface ever so shiny.
But I can only glue myself back together so many times
before I fall apart completely.
And when I do, you will know.
You will see what you truly meant to me.
You will know I was collateral damage to your damaged self.
You will understand how broken you have made me.
Just maybe, when you see this brokenness,
you will decide to pick up my pieces.
Gluing me back together.
And if you don't, I will finally have the courage to move on.
I will bounce back, knowing I was bold enough to make a statement.
I will never wonder what might have been.
Never again to be haunted by the what if.
What if I neglected to show you how much you consumed me?
How much you still consume me.
How much I still want to be consumed by you.

Have you ever loved someone for the simplest of reasons?
These miniscule moments that aren't so miniscule at all.
Creating a never-ending pounding in your heart.
With each encounter, your heart races a little faster.
Faster and faster until it feels as though it might burst,
but by some miracle it continues to beat on.
Leaving you to wonder if their heart beats to the same rhythm.
Do they ever think of you?
Would you stand a chance?
Every once in a while love taps you on the shoulder.
Dropping hints that there is potential for more.
More to these little moments.
More than what meets the eye.
More than a regular life, but a beautiful life.
A life made up of a million little moments.
Love always challenges us.
Puts obstacles in the way of what we want.
The risk of heartbreak, as well as the chance for love.
Convincing ourselves to enjoy moments we have been given.
Unable to risk it all, to risk having nothing at all.
But what if?
What if we are accepted by the other person?
Accepted for the love we now share together.
A lifetime of love.
See, that's the crazy thing about love.
It's one or the other.
It's with or without that one person.
Without them, what do we have?
A forced friendship.
Even the thought of that repulses you.
Once rejected by that type of love, being friends is out of the question.
Then there is the other side of the spectrum.
You grow in your love for each other.
Through the good and the bad.
Nurturing the mutual feelings.
Love is completely insane like that.
It's one or the other, with no in between.
So you ask yourself...
Is the risk of having absolutely nothing worth the possibility of everything?

I'm going to finish my story today.
I bet you're all thinking I ended up with this person.
The person I saw once upon a time across the crowded room.
It would be perfect, would it not?
This hidden spark that transformed into a fire of everlasting love.
I am sorry to tell you, but that is not how this story is going to end.
At first I didn't know where I was going with this.
If it would lead to something worth sharing.
Something magical.
A fairy tale of sorts.
But that's not always how love—or life, as a matter of fact—works.
It's not always going to be easy.
It's not always going to be glorious.
And it's most definitely not always going to be what you want it to be.
This story does not have a happy ending.
The prince charming in this tale didn't have the guts
to ask the princess to the ball.
And this princess did not have the time to wait around.
But maybe I don't want to be a princess after all.
Maybe I just want to be a girl who falls in love with a guy.
A guy who will appear when I least expect it.

You.
A face on the boardgame of *Guess Who.*
My opponent, the future, guides me toward you.
Dropping hints.
Watching me as I choose the faces I hope to be you.
The only problem is, I don't know who you are.
But at the same time I do.
You are the person I watch sunsets with from the back of my truck.
You are the boy I force to the dance floor as *Sweet Child O' Mine* comes on.
You are the companion to many nights with your favourite stargazing girl.
You are the individual that gets me in bed with my secret turn-ons.
You are the laugh I hear when I make a fool of my clumsy self.
You are the being I listen to for hours on end about the most random of things.
You are the one I want to be young and dumb with.
You are the man I see as I turn to walk down the aisle.
You are the husband that travels the world with his world.
You are the father that teaches our children right from wrong.
You are the grandfather that volunteers his time to babysit.
You are the old man I fall in love with each and every day.
You are the mystery I cannot wait to discover.

As I reminiscence through my time lost in love,
I realize I was neither lost nor in love.
I was in love with the idea of love.
Infatuated.
Falling for a vision.
Time and time again buying what others sold.
Unable to see their products were empty promises.
I was in denial.
Stuck in a trance I could not shake.
Enchanted by the future I thought they could give me.
Denying myself the right to admit my picture-perfect world wasn't so perfect.
And now I am scared.
Scared of the one.
My lips unsure they will be able to admit their truth.
Fearful I have met yet another double agent.

LOST & FOUND

I have walked blindly in the unforgiveable forest far too long.
Lost in the dark crevasses of forgotten trees.
Leaving my emotions vulnerable to the demons
that lurk at their roots and above my head in the branches.
I find myself walking in circles.
Seeing the same surroundings time and time again.
Unable to map my way out of the shadows.
On occasion, light trickles through the leaves.
As I finish my ascent toward the shining light,
completing my climb up the trunk of the wise oak,
my head pierces through the crown of the tree.
To my dismay, the view shows no sign of the forest's edge.
So I continue to venture indefinitely through the woods.
That is, until one day, I reach a clearing.
At first, I think I must be dreaming.
Visualizing a temporary mirage.
My eyes tampering with my mind.
For reassurance, I pinch myself.
Still uncertain the open field in front of me is real.
Unable to believe I have finally reached my haven.
I was once lost and now I have been found.
Found by you.

Here's to *Cinderella, The Notebook, P.S I Love You, Notting Hill, Romeo and Juliet.*
Selling me a plot I never dreamed to be true.
Allowing me to believe in romance a little less
with each attempt to direct my own love life.
With each attempt to leap into the arms of Patrick Swayze,
I fell shorter and shorter from landing the perfect jump.
With each attempt Adam Sandler made to flirt with me over tipi waffles,
I grew further from remembering him the next morning at breakfast.
With each attempt to become a pretty woman fit for Richard Gere's riches,
I found I could not buy enough clothes
or makeup in the world to cover my true self.
I could not care less.
I no longer envy the movies.
I don't need them, because I have you.
I get to live in my own romantic motion picture every day.
Today.
Tomorrow.
And for the rest of my life.
P.S. I still love you, rom coms... I just love my man more.

It's in the eyes.
The way they look at me.
Light blue, followed by a fierce grey.
The way they fixate on me as you shake your head back and forth.
In complete disbelief that I am yours.
The way I look back at them.
Paired with an idiotic smile I can never seem to wipe off my face.
It's all in the eyes.
That's how you know.
They tell the whole story.
The story of us.
How, once upon a time, I looked into those magnificent eyes.
And how I sit here now, promising to stare into them happily ever after.

“I feel like I’ve known you from the second I met you.”
Now, don’t quote me on that,
but that is the gist of what was said over pillow talk.
Who are you?
How did you come to exist?
Can I study you in a science lab?
If so, does anyone know the best way to clone a human?
Jk sexy, I promise I’m crazy.
*not crazy
Funny how I accidently forgot to mention the “not” just then.
You are probably wondering what is happening to me.
Why this piece is, to put it nicely, spiraling into a shit storm.
She’s not making sense.
Call for help.
Get her a chill pill.
Or don’t.
Let me stay on this high.
This high I like to call loveeeeeeeeee.
Keep’ er coming.
I’ll pay my plug whatever they want to have you on supply.
If they don’t, I can promise you the withdrawals will be a bitch.
Cuz I’m addicted and I just can’t get enough; I just can’t get enough.

I have an unfailing trust in us.
I no longer require a title to justify the relationship.
We are not definable by a thing, talking, dating,
boyfriend and girlfriend, fiancés, husband and wife.
We are two people together for all the right reasons,
even when they feel wrong.
Choosing to cut out any stipulations.
Rejecting the need for a contract.
Understanding that love is not a business.
Driven by an intention you set for each other with each new day.
Unwavering in what we found.
Never manipulated by the thought of what could be lost.

I love the way you glance over at me before a picture is taken.
I love when you literally and figuratively sweep me off my feet.
I love how you shake your head and stare at me while you tell me I'm beautiful.
I love walking into my room to find a secret message left on my whiteboard.
I love that we can laugh at how we are complete and utter goofballs.
I love when you end a text with a stick winky face instead of an emoji.
I love how much I love you.

Love is sappy.
Sappy in more ways than one.
First, there is the cheesy romantic type.
The tear jerking, all or nothing moments.
A time for light and fluffy.
Then you have the kind of sappy forged from maple trees.
Sticking to your hands as would glue.
A necessary, yet annoying, component of syrup production.
The one flaw to the magnificent maple tree.
Still, despite this, we choose to love it.
We choose to love it because love is sappy.
Not always sappy as described in our first definition.
Similar to maple syrup's reliance on sap.
Once boiled, this adhesive substance transforms into a sweet treat.
However, one cannot exist without the other.
Love is choosing to appreciate the person as a whole.
The sap and the syrup.

The words that leave your mouth never felt so clear entering my ears.
Speaking to me in a language that I can finally understand.
Silencing the foreign tongues that surround me.
Starving the urge I feel to learn their form of dialect.
Finally, I can throw my translation book away in the garbage with confidence.
When I am with you, communication comes with ease.
Each syllable acting to reassure the fate that brought us together.
I was deaf.
Failing in my attempts to read lips.
Losing my will to follow along with the subtitles.
Struggling to comprehend my inability to grasp sign language.
Then came you.
An answer amidst a lifetime of neglected questions.

Finding the one is like training for a run.
It takes time.
Effort.
Patience.
It takes perseverance.
A strong will to reach your goal.
A commitment to training.
Obstacles that get in the way of said training.
In my case, it was a half marathon.
My prize waiting for me at the finish line was you.
A new-found stranger cheering me on.
A stranger I never want to unknow.
A stranger I plan to spend the rest of my life running after.

Although I have yet to see the whole wide world,
I have seen enough to know you are my world.
Knowing home is to know the world.
To see it all and know where you belong.
To know when you feel your best.
To know what makes you wake up every morning.
To know who will always have a place in your heart.
To know why life is worth living.
To know how no one person, place, or thing will measure up to being with them.
The world is not measured by the number of footprints you leave on this earth.
Rather, by the number of seconds you get to spend with those you love most.

"Don't let me hold you back from living your dreams."
Baby, you are my dream.
You're the boy I used to fill my diaries with as a little girl.
You're the reason I wake up from nightmares unfazed.
You're the man hiding under those sheets of shining armour.
You're the only cause I would ever deem worth fighting for.
You're the first thing I want to see when I wake up.
You're the last person I need to say "I love you" to at day's end.
You're the dream that exists whether I am asleep or not.

THE GOLDEN RULES

Swan Street is known for its high speed traffic.
One of few roads in my small town that always seems to be busy.
Conveniently, my childhood house was located on said street.
The driveway had an aggressive curve that landed directly on the road.
Let's just say that learning how to ride my first bike was a do or die situation.
When I was young, I remember holding my mom's hand on the sidewalk's edge.
Every time before we crossed,
she would glance over at me and say "What are the golden rules?"
This question was brought to life in threatening situations,
similar to the one stated above,
in the hope that I would know the answer.
Acting with the intention to mold me into a responsible adult.
As I matured, my house, age, personality, and so on changed.
But the golden rules never did.
Rather, they developed, as did I.
A combination of what I took from my mother as well as my own experiences.
Developing into the rules I live by today.
Rules that I intend to live out for the rest of my life,
no matter how young or old I may be.

In life, we make choices.
While some seem smaller than others,
all have relevance in shaping the person we are to become.
Bringing with them opportunity, potential, self discovery, change, and growth.
Acting to challenge our past selves to be present.
Present for the decisions to come.
Understanding that each one shapes you as a person.
For better or worse,
action had to be taken.
While some choices are reached at gunpoint,
others drag out as would a slow motion bullet clip from an action movie.
No matter the timeframe,
choose your path wisely.
Everything counts for something.

The toxic people of your past are similar to a favourite toy.
Or rather, once treasured.
Aging back to the time of childhood memories.
Now tucked away in storage for safe keeping.
Acting to distance yourself from Mr. Snuggles the bear.
No longer seeking protection from under your beloved blankie.
Maturing from your days spent with Barbie and her luxurious lifestyle.
You cannot find the energy to take a gamble with Monopoly.
Growing too tall to hide behind the walls of your Lego blocks.
How is it that these innocent toys compare to the demons of one's past?
Acceptance.
Understanding when the time has come to let go of our stuffed companions.
What used to benefit you no longer serves a purpose.
What brought comfort will only exist to hold you back.
What once unleashed imagination now traps your ability to live in reality.
In order to grow, there comes a time when the toy chest must close indefinitely.

Friends are the family we choose.
This leaves me to wonder...
Would I have chosen my family members
as friends if we had not been related?
It's crazy to think how powerful a bond is formed between family.
No matter what they may do or say,
you will always love them.
We may not always admit it to each other,
but without each other, we know that life would be unbelievably difficult.
Family doesn't always mean being related by blood.
Maybe you are related through the life experiences
and challenges you face together.
It's a lifetime of never-ending love and a forever-growing connection.
Family is unbreakable and constantly being redefined.
Family is family, it's as simple and beautiful as that.
They are your friends for life.

Waiting.
Waiting for the final destination of a long journey.
Waiting for the answer to a twisted mystery.
Waiting for the silver lining that needs to result from this pain.
Waiting for an opportunity to sweep you off your feet.
The seconds feel like hours, and hours like days.
Time plays a taunting game with us,
laughing at our struggle to remain patient.
But maybe time is not doing so to be cruel.
But rather to teach us how to appreciate each and every moment.
Allowing us to acknowledge the work necessary to reach a desired goal.
If we were constantly given things in life, it would be too easy.
Stripping us of our sense of purpose and drive.
Time kindly forces us to see all that life consists of.
Reminding us to seize the moment,
no matter what that may be.
The bad and the good.
The trenches and mountaintops.
The darkness and the light.

Being a mediator has its pros and cons.
Attempting to support all individuals involved.
Convincing yourself this role ensures a drama-free life.
Lying to yourself as the bullets whiz by.
An idiot waving a white flag in the middle of a raging war.
Will it be that some drop their guns and follow you,
replacing their weapons with peace offerings?
Or you get shot on your mission to bring opposing sides together?
Maybe you arrive to the battlefield too late.
All that remains is a field overrun by poppies
fertilized by the bodies of fallen soldiers.
Choose your battles wisely.
Certain people or passions may be worth fighting for.
However, you might be able to cure this argument with peace.
Perhaps sometimes the only action that can be taken is to walk away.
To know when the risks outweigh the benefits.
To know when you will become collateral damage
to a fight that was never yours to begin with.
Let go of the little things in life as a means to focus on the true task at hand.
You can only engage yourself in so many pointless battles
before you lose your will to fight for what really matters.

Don't rush love.
Take time to be independent.
Take time to understand who you are without a significant other.
Take time to love yourself.
One day, you will fall deeply in love with someone.
You will find the person you never want to say goodbye to.
You will have the opportunity to put your heart on the line in the name of love.
Until then, take advantage of the time you have been given to be you.
You need to know who you are before you can know another.
Don't rush individuality.

Words possess power.
A strength unlike any other.
Each letter, syllable, phrase, sentence,
forming to create a point.
Despite our efforts to entrap them,
they will find a means to escape.
Eating away at our insides until they reach the surface.
Leading you to release the burdened feelings that lie below.
A secret love that wishes to be shared with the world.
An overstretched lie that cries out in desperation to reveal itself.
A quiet voice that pleads to speak up against evil.
No matter the reason,
thoughts were not formed to be silenced.
Speak up.
Life is short.
You will live to regret the things you didn't say.

Determination.
Our will to get the job done.
To give up or push onward?
Convincing ourselves the goal in sight is unreachable.
Underqualified for the task at hand.
Unable to find time to complete the work.
Undeserving of a shot at such a life.
However, we have the potential to live the dream.
Unfortunately, we also possess the ability to find a reason not to do something.
Reasons to ignore our talent.
Reasons not to take a risk.
Reasons to accept the ordinary.

A wise woman once told me "A weed is a plant in an unwanted area."
A plant without a purpose.
A parallel concept to the unnecessary people in our life.
Failure to eliminate said weeds will act to suffocate the roots that lie below.
Stripping them of their rightful space to grow.
Although these weeds may have a reason to exist elsewhere,
elsewhere is not where you need to be.
The plant is nothing more than a tap on the shoulder misleading us to turn back.
Preventing their victims from discovering the world in front of them.
We must determine for ourselves
when a plant is the beauty and when it is the beast.
A radiant rose, when placed in a glass display, will inevitably wither away.
Drowning the belle in oxygen
until the final petal has fallen to the belly of the encasement.

Listen to your body.
Think of it as a parent.
A parent nagging you to make your bed at the crack of dawn.
Pointing their finger at the dreaded corner chair to cue for a time out.
Staring at you impatiently as you fiddle with the peas at dinner.
You, the child, attempting to avoid punishment by all means necessary.
Unable to see that their words of wisdom come from a place of compassion.
Unable to understand that they have nothing but the best intentions for you.
Unable to determine when it is time to accept their forced love.
Listen to your body.
It wants you to succeed.

Picture this.
A caterpillar finds himself on a path.
A dangerously long venture through the forest.
Followed by a leaf ride along the river.
His bug buddies back home grow worrisome.
Unsure where their companion has wandered off to.
Little do they know, their furry friend is on the quest of a lifetime.
Facing experiences unlike any other.
Losing himself in the mystery of it all.
That is, until he finds himself dangling upside down from a branch.
Falling into a deep slumber.
Days later, the creatures back home meet a radiant butterfly.
"Where have you journeyed from, Mr. Butterfly?" they ask.
The butterfly looks at them in disbelief.
"Why, it is me, of course," he replies.
He continues, after receiving blank faces in response,
by saying "Carder the Caterpillar."
The critters look at each other hesitantly.
As the conversation continues,
they realize he is speaking the truth.
In doing so, they raise their many legs and wings in celebration.
Carder, still unsure who this "Mr. Butterfly" is,
joins in the community's enthusiasm.
If only innocent Carder knew what he had become.
Self-change happens without our knowing.
Similar to that of this classic children's tale.

Honesty is gold.
A neglected set of bricks.
Deposited into a bank.
Waiting in the hopes that it will grow to fulfill the owner's needs.
Left to collect dust in a safe.
Preventing the riches from being reached by the poor.
Kept locked away.
As a means of protection from any unworthy thieves.
The cobwebs that collect lies will inevitably be walked through to reveal the truth.
Supressing the truth will only fester unhealthy relationships.
Dishonesty to one's self and those around them
will result in stolen time with people they truly love.

Love takes courage.
Love takes sacrifice.
Love takes patience.
Never-ending and pure and on its own agenda.
Love will always find a way back,
no matter how dangerous the road ahead may be.
No matter what we may want to believe,
it is always there.
We live for it.
A power beyond any physical strength.
As life-giving as the air that passes through our lungs.
Breathe in the love.
Breathe it out to others.

You have to recognize when it is time to pick yourself up.
You cannot always depend on others.
Everyone is going through a battle of their own,
fighting to stay on their own two feet.
Helping another individual to find balance is beyond them.
Always lend a helping hand when you feel stable,
remembering kindness was a choice you made...
Keeping in mind it is not always a two-way street.
Sometimes you have to be your own hero, and they have to be theirs.
Get back up.
You are resilient.
Keep fighting.
You've got this!

Never give up on the things you love most.
Finding your passion in life allows you to live life to the fullest.
The moment you realize your true passion,
everything else gets a little clearer.
Life never ends up being what you expected,
but isn't that half the excitement?
Human beings are always searching for a purpose.
Sometimes we simply have to wait for it to come our way.
Passions can range from a career,
to the care of another person,
to fighting for what you believe in.
In many cases, we often put our passions to the side,
but maybe we need to learn how to prioritize our passions.
So many of us get caught up in everything else
and lose sight of what matters most.
Many of us cannot live off our dreams,
because at the end of the day we need to have enough money
to feed and shelter ourselves.
Why can't we have both?
I constantly wonder what life would look like
if I were able to write while living comfortably.
I want to live the dream.
Don't we all?
I'm going to chase my passion and fight for what I love,
so that one day maybe I can live the dream.
Fight for your purpose and live for your passion.
You never know where it might take you...

Two is better than one.
Sure, we need time to be alone,
but some things are simply better together.
Would you rather they read the story of your life,
or accept your invitation to live it with you.
Would you rather watch the mountaintop view by yourself,
or create a memory while climbing it with a fellow hiker?
Would you rather video chat loved ones from across the world,
or decide to love them sitting by your side?
Would you rather hear the laughter of strangers around you,
or produce a genuine laugh with someone you share a connection with?
I dare you to find yourself,
keeping in mind the pieces of you that come from others.

We constantly allow ourselves to believe that life is
made up of temporary moments of happiness.
That the future will only lead to disappointment.
So we choose to save ourselves from the pain we predict.
Relieving our future selves from the heartbreak, the letdown, the sorrow.
However, could this be our very problem?
If we consistently anticipate failure, that is what we shall receive.
We are all susceptible to getting hurt.
This does not mean we must live out entire lives in fear.
If we are to have a shot at greatness, we must first learn how to take risks.
Stand against the odds.
Take a chance.
Be open to the possibilities.
Put yourself out to the universe,
and just maybe it will give you something in return.

The Philosopher's Stone called to me from the library shelves,
daring my ten-year-old self to explore the world of witchcraft and wizardry.
Commencing nights on end of relentless reading
as I followed in the footsteps of a young boy to a mysterious castle.
From the chocolate frog on the Hogwarts Express
to the humble centaur of the Forbidden Forest,
I found myself lost in J.K. Rowling's masterpiece.
The words putting me under a deep spell.
My eyes unable to strip themselves from the pages of the novel,
until I was ready to read the next.
Until there was no longer a next to read.
However, the magic lived on.
Through the visits to the theatre every year a new movie was released.
Through play with friends carving wands
and attending potion classes in my back yard.
Through the rereading of my favourite chapters on rainy days.
That is, until the enchantment wore off.
My collection of seven slowly accumulating with dust.
Sitting ever so patiently on a bookshelf of lost dreams.
Awaiting the opportunity to release the magic
from behind their neglected covers once again.
This, my fellow muggles, is how it feels to grow up.

I've always felt out of place,
in search of something better.
I have come to realize that the search is not to discover a physical place,
but rather a place within yourself and those around you.
This can be achieved in one of two ways.
Either change something within yourself,
or eliminate the negativity around you.
Life is incredible no matter where it takes you.
You may just have to dig a little deeper to reach it.
Dig in the places that few would dare to look.
Dig through the outside barriers of another individual
to find an outstanding person.
Dig to reveal the true and simple meanings in life.
Many of us simply see what lies on the surface.
Never exposing ourselves to the roots stretching long and far below.
I dare you to pick up a shovel and start digging.
You never know what you might find below the surface.

So this is life...
A book that will act to reassure your existence.
Acting to expose what the dot dot dot failed to deliver.
Acting to complete the unfinished sentence.
Acting to give reasoning to this thing we all call life.
But how wrong you are.
Although it may seem I have put in my two cents worth,
I'm still not so sure myself.
Not so sure if there is a punchline.
Not so sure if there is an answer to justify what life is.
Not so sure if I want to figure it out at all.
Why should we need to define it,
when we can choose, instead, to live it?
I ask you to grasp every second.
To see all there is to see.
To be a somebody to someone.
To give life a chance to show you that no words can describe what it truly is.

Made in the USA
Monee, IL
21 March 2020

23613199R00113